First World War
and Army of Occupation
War Diary
France, Belgium and Germany

29 DIVISION
Divisional Troops
Divisional Trench Mortar Batteries
1 August 1916 - 31 January 1919

WO95/2292/3

The Naval & Military Press Ltd
www.nmarchive.com
Published in association with The National Archives

Published by

The Naval & Military Press Ltd

Unit 10 Ridgewood Industrial Park,

Uckfield, East Sussex,

TN22 5QE England

Tel: +44 (0) 1825 749494

www.naval-military-press.com

www.nmarchive.com

This diary has been reprinted in facsimile from the original. Any imperfections are inevitably reproduced and the quality may fall short of modern type and cartographic standards.

© Crown Copyright
Images reproduced by permission of The National Archives, London, England, 2015.

Contents

Document type	Place/Title	Date From	Date To
Heading	WO95/2292/3 Divisional Trench Mortar Batteries		
Heading	29th Division. Troops Trench Mortar Batteries Aug 1916-Jan 1919		
Heading	29th Division. "S" 29 Trench Mortar Battery August 1916		
War Diary	Mailly Maillet	01/08/1916	31/08/1916
Heading	29th Division. 'V' 29 Heavy Trench Mortar Battery August 1916		
War Diary	Hamel	21/08/1916	30/08/1916
Heading	29th Division. "Z" 29 Trench Mortar Battery August 1916		
War Diary	Beaumont	01/08/1916	01/08/1916
War Diary	Hamel Sector	02/08/1916	02/08/1916
War Diary	Somme	03/08/1916	04/08/1916
War Diary	Amplier	05/08/1916	05/08/1916
War Diary	Pas de Calais	15/08/1916	15/08/1916
War Diary	Beaumont	16/08/1916	16/08/1916
War Diary	Hamel Sector	17/08/1916	19/08/1916
War Diary	Beaumont	20/08/1916	20/08/1916
War Diary	Hamel Sector	21/08/1916	28/08/1916
War Diary	Beaumont	29/08/1916	29/08/1916
War Diary	Hamel Sector	30/08/1916	30/08/1916
Heading	29th Division. "V" 29 Heavy Trench Mortar Battery September 1916		
Heading	War Diary Of V29 H.T.M.B. From 1.9.16 To 29.9.16 Volume No		
War Diary	Hamel	01/09/1916	02/09/1916
War Diary	Mailly-Maillet	03/09/1916	07/09/1916
War Diary	Louvencourt	08/09/1916	10/09/1916
War Diary	Field	11/09/1916	11/09/1916
War Diary	Poperinghe	12/09/1916	15/09/1916
War Diary	Ypres	16/09/1916	29/09/1916
War Diary	Casualties To Accompany A F C 2118 29 H.T		
Heading	29th Division. "X" 29 Trench Mortar Battery September 1916		
Heading	War Diary Of X/29 T.M.B. From 1-9-16 To 30/9/16 Volume No 2		
War Diary	Hamel	01/09/1916	01/09/1916
War Diary	Martinsart	02/09/1916	08/09/1916
War Diary	Louvencourt	09/09/1916	10/09/1916
War Diary	Belle Eglise	10/09/1916	11/09/1916
War Diary	Poperinghe	12/09/1916	15/09/1916
War Diary	Ypres	16/09/1916	30/09/1916
Heading	29th Division. "Y" 29 Trench Mortar Battery September 1916		
Heading	War Diary Of Y/29 T.M.B. From 24-9-16 To 30/9/16 Volume No 2		
War Diary	Ypres	24/09/1916	30/09/1916
Heading	29th Division. "Z" 29 Trench Mortar Battery September 1916		

Heading	War Diary Of Z/29 T.M.B. From 1-9-16 To 30/9/16		
War Diary	In The Field	03/09/1916	27/09/1916
Heading	29th Division. "V" 29 Heavy Trench Mortar Battery October 1916		
Heading	War Diary Of V29 H. T. H. B. From 1st October 1916 To 30th October 1916 Volume		
War Diary	Ypres	01/10/1916	14/10/1916
War Diary	S22 C	15/10/1916	15/10/1916
War Diary	S22C7070	16/10/1916	30/10/1916
Miscellaneous			
Heading	29th Division. "X" 29 Trench Mortar Battery October 1916		
Heading	War Diary Of 207/29th Trench Mortar Battery RA From 1st October 1916 To 31st October 1916 Volume 3		
War Diary	Ypres	30/09/1916	07/10/1916
War Diary	Esquelbecq	07/10/1916	09/10/1916
War Diary	Daours	10/10/1916	11/10/1916
War Diary	Camp "A"	12/10/1916	16/10/1916
War Diary	Bazentin	17/10/1916	30/10/1916
War Diary	Albert	31/10/1916	31/10/1916
Heading	29th Division. "Y" 29 Trench Mortar Battery October 1916		
Heading	War Diary Of Y/29th Trench Mortar Battery R.A. From 1st October 1916 To 31st October 1916 Volume 3		
War Diary	Ypres	30/09/1916	08/10/1916
War Diary	Esquebec	09/10/1916	10/10/1916
War Diary	Douars	11/10/1916	12/10/1916
War Diary	Albert	13/10/1916	13/10/1916
War Diary	Camp	14/10/1916	15/10/1916
War Diary	12th Div. Dump	16/10/1916	20/10/1916
War Diary	Flers	23/10/1916	25/10/1916
War Diary	Camps 15.a	26/10/1916	28/10/1916
War Diary	Flers	29/10/1916	30/10/1916
War Diary	Albert	31/10/1916	31/10/1916
Heading	29th Division. "Z" 29 Trench Mortar Battery October 1916		
War Diary	War Diary Of Z/29th Trench Mortar Batteries R.A. From 1st October 1916 To 31st October 1916 Volume 3		
Heading	War Diary Of Z 29 Trench Mortar Battery From 1st Oct To 31st 16 (Volume)		
War Diary	In The Field	01/10/1916	31/10/1916
Heading	29th Division. "V" 29 Heavy Trench Mortar Battery November 1916		
Heading	War Diary Of V/29 Heavy Trench Mortar Battery From 1st Nov 1916 To 30th Nov 1916 (Volume)		
War Diary	Quarry A.M. Dump.	01/11/1916	25/11/1916
War Diary	E27a10 10	26/11/1916	27/11/1916
War Diary	Daours	28/11/1916	30/11/1916
Miscellaneous	Casualty Report To Accompany A.F.C. 2118 War Diary November 1916	29/11/1916	29/11/1916
Heading	29th Division. "X" 29 Trench Mortar Battery November 1916		
Heading	War Diary Of X/29 Trench Mortar Battery From 1st Nov 1916 To 30th Nov 1916. (Volume No 4)		
Miscellaneous	Headquarters 29th Div Arty	06/12/1916	06/12/1916
War Diary	Albert	01/11/1916	13/11/1916

War Diary	Daours	14/11/1916	30/11/1916
Heading	29th Division. "Y" 29 Trench Mortar Battery November 1916		
Heading	War Diary Of Y/29 Trench Mortar Battery From 1st Nov 1916 To 30th Nov 1916 (Volume No 4)		
War Diary	Albert	01/11/1916	13/11/1916
War Diary	Daours	14/11/1916	30/11/1916
Heading	29th Division. "Z" 29 Trench Mortar Battery November 1916		
Heading	War Diary Of Z/29 Trench Mortar Battery From 1st Nov 1916 To 30th Nov 1916 (Volume)		
War Diary	In The Field	01/11/1916	30/11/1916
Heading	29th Division. 29th Division. "V" 29 Heavy Trench Mortar Battery December 1916		
War Diary	War Diary Of V/29 (Heavy) Trench Mortar Battery From 1st December 1916 To 31st December 1916 (Volume)		
War Diary	Daours (France)	01/12/1916	11/12/1916
War Diary	Carnoy	12/12/1916	29/12/1916
War Diary	Casualty Report V. 29 H.J.M.B. To Accompany A.F.C. 2118 War Diary Dec 1916		
Heading	29th Division. "X" 29 Trench Mortar Battery December 1916		
Miscellaneous	X 29 Trench Mortar Bty 7-2-17	07/02/1917	07/02/1917
Miscellaneous	Headquarters 29 Division A	11/02/1917	11/02/1917
War Diary	Daours	01/12/1916	11/12/1916
War Diary	Pommiers	12/12/1916	12/12/1916
War Diary	Redoubt	24/12/1916	24/12/1916
War Diary	Camp	25/12/1916	26/12/1916
War Diary	Vaux	27/12/1916	31/12/1916
Heading	29th Division. "Y" 29 Trench Mortar Battery December 1916		
Heading	War Diary Of Y/29 Trench Mortar Battery From 1st December 1916 To 31st December 1916 (Volume 5)		
War Diary	Daours	01/12/1916	11/12/1916
War Diary	Pomerier Redoubt	12/12/1916	31/12/1916
Heading	29th Division. "Z" 29 Trench Mortar Battery December 1916		
Heading	War Diary Of Z/29 Trench Mortar Battery From 1st December 1916 To 31st December 1916 (Volume)		
War Diary	In The Field	01/12/1916	31/12/1916
Heading	War Diary Of V/29 Heavy Trench Mortar Battery From 1st January 1917 To 31st January 1917 (Volume 6)		
War Diary	Carnoy (Somme)	01/01/1917	16/01/1917
War Diary	Combles	17/01/1917	31/01/1917
Miscellaneous	Casualty Report V.2.9 H.J.M.B. To Accompany A.F.C. 2118 (War Diary)	29/01/1917	29/01/1917
Heading	War Diary Of X/29 Trench Mortar Battery From 1st January 1917 To 31st January 1917 (Volume 6)		
War Diary	Vaux	01/01/1917	05/01/1917
War Diary	Morlancourt	06/01/1917	10/01/1917
War Diary	Combles	11/01/1917	17/01/1917
War Diary	Sailly-Saillisel	18/01/1917	20/01/1917
War Diary	Carnoy	21/01/1917	21/01/1917
War Diary	Guillimont	22/01/1917	28/01/1917
War Diary	Pommiers Redoubt	29/01/1917	31/01/1917

Heading	War Diary Of Y/29 Trench Mortar Battery From 1st January 1917 To 31st January 1917 (Volume 6)		
War Diary	Pommiers Redoubt	01/01/1917	02/01/1917
War Diary	Morlancourt	03/01/1917	10/01/1917
War Diary	Combles	11/01/1917	12/01/1917
War Diary	Sailly	13/01/1917	13/01/1917
War Diary	Saillisel	14/01/1917	15/01/1917
War Diary	Combles	16/01/1917	20/01/1917
War Diary	Minden Post	21/01/1917	26/01/1917
War Diary	Pommiers	27/01/1917	31/01/1917
Heading	War Diary Of Z/29 Trench Mortar Battery From 1st January 1917 To 31st January 1917 (Volume 6)		
War Diary	In The Field	01/01/1917	30/01/1917
Heading	War Diary Of V/29 Heavy Trench Mortar Battery From 1st Feby 1917 To 28th Feby 1917 (Volume 7)		
War Diary	Carnoy	01/02/1917	17/02/1917
War Diary	Sailly-Saillisel	18/02/1917	28/02/1917
Miscellaneous	V/29th H.T.M.B. Monthly Casualties To Accompany A.F.C. 2118		
War Diary	Pommiers	01/02/1917	02/02/1917
War Diary	Redoubt	03/02/1917	04/02/1917
War Diary	Camp	05/02/1917	08/02/1917
War Diary	Carnoy	09/02/1917	16/02/1917
War Diary	Sailly	17/02/1917	28/02/1917
Heading	War Diary Of Y/29 Trench Mortar Battery From 1st Feby 1917 To 28th Feby 1917 (Volume No 7)		
War Diary	Carnoy	01/02/1917	05/02/1917
War Diary	Morval	06/02/1917	09/02/1917
War Diary	Carnoy	10/02/1917	12/02/1917
War Diary	Vaux	13/02/1917	24/02/1917
War Diary	Carnoy	25/02/1917	28/02/1917
Heading	War Diary Of Z/29 Trench Mortar Battery From 1st February 1917 To 28th February 1917 (Volume 7)		
War Diary	In The Field	01/02/1917	28/02/1917
Heading	War Diary Of V/29th Heavy Trench Mortar Battery R.A. March 1st 1917 To March 31st 1917. (Volume No 8)		
War Diary	Sailly-Saillisel	01/03/1917	04/03/1917
War Diary	Carnoy	05/03/1917	08/03/1917
War Diary	Morcancourt	08/03/1917	31/03/1917
Miscellaneous	V 29 H.T.M.B. Casualty Return To Accompany A.F.C. 2118 War Diary		
Heading	War Diary Of "X"/29th Trench. Mortar Battery, R.A. March 1st 1917 To March 31st 1917. (Volume: No 8)		
War Diary	Sallisel	01/03/1917	04/03/1917
War Diary	Carnoy	05/03/1917	07/03/1917
War Diary	Morlancourt	08/03/1917	28/03/1917
War Diary	Gourns	29/03/1917	30/03/1917
War Diary	Anar	31/03/1917	31/03/1917
Heading	War Diary "Y"/29th Trench Mortar Battery R.A. March 1st 1917 To March 31st 1917 (Volume: No 8)		
War Diary	Carnoy	01/03/1917	07/03/1917
War Diary	Morlancourt	08/03/1917	22/03/1917
War Diary	Franvillers	23/03/1917	23/03/1917
War Diary	Flesselles	24/03/1917	25/03/1917
War Diary	St Acheul	26/03/1917	26/03/1917

War Diary	Pt Bouret	27/03/1917	27/03/1917
War Diary	Gouves	28/03/1917	29/03/1917
War Diary	Arras	30/03/1917	31/03/1917
Heading	War Diary Of "Z"/29th Trench Mortar Battery, R.A. March 1st 1917 To March, 31st 1917. (Volume: No 8)		
War Diary	In The Field	01/03/1917	31/03/1917
Heading	War Diary Of "V"/29th Heavy Trench Mortar Battery, From: 1st April 1917 To 30th April 1917. (Volume: 9)		
War Diary	Arras	01/04/1917	30/04/1917
Miscellaneous	Casualty Report	30/04/1917	30/04/1917
Heading	War Diary Of X/29th Trench Mortar Battery From:- April 1st 1917 To April 30th 1917		
War Diary	Arras	01/04/1917	30/04/1917
Heading	War Diary Of Y/29th Trench Mortar Battery From:- April 1st 1917 To April 30th 1917. (Volume: No.9)		
War Diary	Arras	01/04/1917	30/04/1917
War Diary	War Diary Of "Z"/29th Trench Mortar Battery From:- April 1st 1917 To April 30th 1917. Volume. No 9		
War Diary	In The Field	01/04/1917	30/04/1917
Heading	War Diary Of V/29th Heavy Trench Mortar Battery R.A. From:- May 1st 1917 To May 31st 1917. Volume No 10		
War Diary	Arras	01/05/1917	31/05/1917
Heading	War Diary Of X/29th Trench Mortar Battery R.A. From May 1st 1917 To May 31st 1917. (Volume: No 10)		
War Diary	Arras	01/05/1917	31/05/1917
Heading	War Diary Of Y/29 Trench Mortar Battery, R.A. From: May 1st 1917 To May 31st 1917. (Volume: No 10).		
War Diary	Arras	01/05/1917	31/05/1917
Heading	War Diary Of Z/29th Trench Mortar Battery R.A. From:- May 1st 1917 To May 31st 1917. (Volume:- No 10)		
War Diary	In The Field	01/05/1917	31/05/1917
Heading	War Diary Of "V"/29th Heavy Trench Mortar Battery R.F.A. From: June 1st 1917 To June 30th 1917. (Volume No: 11)		
War Diary	Arras	05/06/1917	22/06/1917
War Diary	Montenes-Court	23/06/1917	30/06/1917
Heading	War Diary Of X/29th Trench Mortar Battery R.F.A. From: June 1st 1917 To June 30th 1917. (Volume No: 11)		
War Diary	Monchy	01/06/1917	06/06/1917
War Diary	Arras	07/06/1917	11/06/1917
War Diary	Monchy	12/06/1917	17/06/1917
War Diary	Monchy Arras	18/06/1917	21/06/1917
War Diary	Montenescourt	22/06/1917	30/06/1917
Heading	War Diary Of Y/29th Trench Mortar Battery R.F.A. From: June 1st 1917 To June 30th 1917. (Volume No: 11)		
War Diary	Montenescourt	01/06/1917	30/06/1917
Heading	War Diary Of Z/29th Trench Mortar Battery R.F.A. From: June 1st 1917 To June 30th 1917. (Volume No 11).		
War Diary	Monchy	01/06/1917	02/06/1917
War Diary	Arras	03/06/1917	08/06/1917
War Diary	Monchy	09/06/1917	12/06/1917
War Diary	Arras	13/06/1917	21/06/1917

War Diary	Montenescourt	22/06/1917	30/06/1917
Heading	War Diary Of V/29th Heavy Trench Mortar Battery R.F.A. From:- July 1st 1917 To:- July 31st 1917. (Volume No 12)		
War Diary	Herzeele	01/07/1917	03/07/1917
War Diary	A 12b Centrae	04/07/1917	04/07/1917
War Diary	Boesinghe	05/07/1917	31/07/1917
Miscellaneous	Casualty List To Accompany A.F.C. 2118 For Month Of July 1917		
Heading	War Diary Of X/29 Trench Mortar Battery R.F.A. From:- July 1st 1917 To:- July 31st 1917. (Volume No 12)		
War Diary	Montenes Court	01/07/1917	01/07/1917
War Diary	Heozele	02/07/1917	02/07/1917
War Diary	Ondank (Belgium)	03/07/1917	11/07/1917
War Diary	Canal Bank	12/07/1917	18/07/1917
War Diary	Ordank	19/07/1917	23/07/1917
War Diary	Canal Bank	24/07/1917	29/07/1917
War Diary	Ordank	30/07/1917	31/07/1917
Heading	War Diary Of Y/29 Trench Mortar Battery R.F.A. From:- July 1st 1917 To:- July 31st 1917. Volume No 12		
War Diary	Montenes Court	01/07/1917	01/07/1917
War Diary	Hengeela	02/07/1917	03/07/1917
War Diary	Ordank	04/07/1917	31/07/1917
Heading	War Diary Of Z/29 Trench Mortar Battery R.F.A. From:- July 1st 1917 To:- July 31st 1917. (Volume No 12)		
War Diary	Herzeel	01/07/1917	02/07/1917
War Diary	Ordank	03/07/1917	08/07/1917
War Diary	Yser Canal	09/07/1917	17/07/1917
War Diary	Ordank	18/07/1917	21/07/1917
War Diary	Yser Canal	22/07/1917	26/07/1917
War Diary	Ordank	27/07/1917	31/07/1917
Heading	War Diary Of V/29 Heavy Trench Mortar Battery, R.A. From:- August 1st 1917 To: August 31st 1917. (Volume No 13.)		
War Diary	A10b 92 [Sheet 28 NW Belgium	01/08/1917	31/08/1917
War Diary	Singapore Camp	05/08/1917	18/08/1917
War Diary	Stafford Camp	19/08/1917	19/08/1917
Heading	War Diary Of "X"/29 Trench Mortar Battery, R.A. From: August 1st 1917 To August 31st 1917. (Volume No.13.)		
War Diary	(Belgium) Ordank	01/08/1917	31/08/1917
Heading	War Diary Of "Y"/29 Trench Mortar Battery, R.A. From: August 1st 1917 To: August 31st 1917. (Volume No 13.)		
War Diary	Belgium 28 NW A 10b 92 Ordank	01/08/1917	07/08/1917
War Diary	Scamps Proven Area Singapore Camp	08/08/1917	16/08/1917
War Diary	S Camp Proven Area Singapore Cmp	17/08/1917	18/08/1917
War Diary	S Camp Proven Area Stafford Camp	19/08/1917	31/08/1917
Heading	War Diary Of "Z"/29 Trench Mortar Battery, R.A. From: August 1st 1917 To August 31st 1917. (Volume No 13.)		
War Diary	Ondank	01/08/1917	07/08/1917
War Diary	Singapore Camp	08/08/1917	18/08/1917

War Diary	Stafford Camp	19/08/1917	31/08/1917
Heading	War Diary Of V/29 Heavy Trench Mortar Battery R.A. From: September 1st 1917 To September 30th 1917. (Volume No 14)		
War Diary	In The Field Belgium	01/09/1917	29/09/1917
Heading	War Diary Of X/29 Trench Mortar Battery R.A. From: September 1st 1917 To September 30th 1917. Volume No 14.		
War Diary	In The Field Belgium	01/09/1917	30/09/1917
Heading	War Diary Of Y/29 Trench Mortar Battery R.A. From: September 1st 1917 To September 30th 1917. Volume No 14.		
War Diary	Stafford Camp 7b A15 (Sheet 27)	01/09/1917	04/09/1917
War Diary	Stafford Camp	04/09/1917	22/09/1917
War Diary	A 12 B 69 (Sheet 28)	23/09/1917	30/09/1917
Heading	War Diary Of Z/29 Trench Mortar Battery R.A. From: September 1st 1917 To September 30th 1917. Volume No 14.		
War Diary	In The Field Belgium	01/09/1917	30/09/1917
Heading	War Diary Of V/29 Heavy Trench Mortar Battery From October 1st 1917 To October 31st 1917. Volume No 15		
War Diary	In The Field	01/10/1917	23/10/1917
War Diary	Woesten Belgium	01/10/1917	24/10/1917
War Diary	Doullens	25/10/1917	25/10/1917
War Diary	Caumesnil	26/10/1917	29/10/1917
War Diary	Vauxl	30/10/1917	31/10/1917
Heading	War Diary Of X/29 Trench Mortar Battery R.A. From. October 1st 1917 To October 31st 1917. Volume No 15.		
War Diary	Woesten	01/10/1917	23/10/1917
War Diary	Proven	24/10/1917	24/10/1917
War Diary	Doullens	25/10/1917	25/10/1917
War Diary	Caumesnil	26/10/1917	30/10/1917
War Diary	St Leger	31/10/1917	31/10/1917
Heading	War Diary Of Y/29 Trench Mortar Battery R.A. From October 1st 1917 To October 31st 1917. Volume No 15.		
War Diary	Woesten Belgium	01/10/1917	11/10/1917
War Diary	Woesten	12/10/1917	25/10/1917
War Diary	Causmesnil	26/10/1917	30/10/1917
War Diary	St Lenger France Patricia Camp	31/10/1917	31/10/1917
Heading	War Diary Of Z/29 Trench Mortar Battery R.A. From October 1st 1917 To October 31st 1917. Volume No 15		
War Diary	Woesten Belgium	01/10/1917	18/10/1917
War Diary	Woesten	19/10/1917	23/10/1917
War Diary	Proven	24/10/1917	24/10/1917
War Diary	Doullens France	25/10/1917	25/10/1917
War Diary	Caumesnil	26/10/1917	30/10/1917
War Diary	St Leger	31/10/1917	31/10/1917
Heading	War Diary Of V/29 Heavy Trench Mortar Battery R.A. From November 1st 1917 To November 30th 1917. Volume No 16		
War Diary	In The Field	01/11/1917	30/11/1917
Heading	War Diary Of X/29 Trench Mortar Battery R.A. From: November 1st 1917 To November 30th 1917. Volume No 16		

War Diary	St Ledger	01/11/1917	23/11/1917
War Diary	Etncourt	24/11/1917	26/11/1917
War Diary	Villers Plouich	27/11/1917	30/11/1917
Heading	War Diary Of Y/29 Trench Mortar Battery R.A. From:- November 1st 1917 To November 30th 1917. Volume No 16.		
War Diary	Patricia's Camp	01/11/1917	23/11/1917
War Diary	Etrecourt	24/11/1917	27/11/1917
War Diary	Villers Plouich	28/11/1917	30/11/1917
Heading	War Diary Of Z/29 Trench Mortar Battery R.A. From:- November 1st 1917 To November 30th 1917. Volume No 16.		
War Diary	St Ledger	01/11/1917	22/11/1917
War Diary	Etricourt	23/11/1917	30/11/1917
War Diary	In The Field	01/12/1917	31/12/1917
Heading	War Diary Of V/29 Heavy Trench Mortar Battery R.A. From: December 1st 1917 To: December 31st 1917. Volume No 17.		
War Diary	In The Field	01/12/1917	31/12/1917
Heading	War Diary Of Y/29 Trench Mortar Battery R.A. From: December 1st 1917 To December 31st 1917. Volume No 17.		
War Diary	Etricourt	01/12/1917	14/12/1917
War Diary	Treux	15/12/1917	17/12/1917
War Diary	Acheux	18/12/1917	23/12/1917
War Diary	Equenicourt	24/12/1917	24/12/1917
War Diary	Maresquel	25/12/1917	31/12/1917
Heading	War Diary Of Z/29 Trench Mortar Battery R.A. From: December 1st 1917 To December 31st 1917. Volume No 17.		
War Diary	In The Field	01/12/1917	31/12/1917
Heading	War Diary Of V/29 Heavy Trench Mortar Battery R.A. From: January 1st 1918 To: January 31st 1918 Volume No 18		
War Diary	In The Field	01/01/1918	31/01/1918
Heading	War Diary Of X/29 Trench Mortar Battery R.A. From: January 1st 1918 To: January 31st 1918 Volume No 18		
War Diary		01/01/1918	31/01/1918
Heading	War Diary Of Y/29 Trench Mortar Battery R.A. From: January 1st 1918: To: January 31st 1918 Volume No 18		
War Diary	Maresquel	01/01/1918	04/01/1918
War Diary	Merk St Levin	05/01/1918	13/01/1918
War Diary	Poperinghe	14/01/1918	19/01/1918
War Diary	Vlamertinghe	20/01/1918	31/01/1918
Heading	War Diary Of Z/29 Trench Mortar Battery R.A. From: January 1st 1918 To: January 31st 1918 Volume No 18		
War Diary	Maresquel	01/01/1918	04/01/1918
War Diary	Merck St Lievin	05/01/1918	10/01/1918
War Diary	Renescure	11/01/1918	11/01/1918
War Diary	Oudezeele	12/01/1918	12/01/1918
War Diary	Poperinghe	13/01/1918	19/01/1918
War Diary	Vlamertinghe	20/01/1918	20/01/1918
War Diary	Wielje Corner	21/01/1918	22/01/1918
War Diary	Vlamertinghe	23/01/1918	25/01/1918
War Diary	Bellevue	25/01/1918	28/01/1918
War Diary	Vlamertinghe	29/01/1918	31/01/1918

Heading	War Diary Of X/29 Trench Mortar Battery R.A. From: February 1st 1918: To February 28th 1918 Volume No 19		
War Diary	Vlamertinghe	01/02/1918	04/02/1918
War Diary	St Jean	04/02/1918	13/02/1918
War Diary	Poperinghe	14/01/1918	28/01/1918
Heading	War Diary Of Y/29 Trench Mortar Battery, R.A. From: February 1st 1918: To February 28th 1918 Volume No 19.		
War Diary	Bellevue	01/02/1918	01/02/1918
War Diary	Vlamertinghe	01/02/1918	05/02/1918
War Diary	Bellevue	05/02/1918	06/02/1918
War Diary	Vlamertinghe	06/02/1918	07/02/1918
War Diary	Bellevue	08/02/1918	08/02/1918
War Diary	Vlamertinghe	09/02/1918	09/02/1918
War Diary	Bellevue	10/02/1918	13/02/1918
War Diary	Vlamertinghe	14/02/1918	14/02/1918
War Diary	Poperinghe	15/02/1918	28/02/1918
Heading	War Diary Of Z/29 Trench Mortar Battery, R.A. From February 1st 1918 To February 28th 1918 Volume No 19		
War Diary	Vlamertinghe	01/02/1918	01/02/1918
War Diary	Bellevue	01/02/1918	01/02/1918
War Diary	Vlamertinghe	02/02/1918	04/02/1918
Heading	War Diary Of V/29 Heavy Trench Mortar Battery R.A. From: February 1st 1918 To: February 28th 1918 Volume No 19		
War Diary	St Jean	01/02/1918	04/02/1918
Heading	War Diary Of X/29 T.M.B. R.A. From March 1st 1918 To March 31st 1918 Volume 20		
War Diary	Poperinghe	01/03/1917	08/03/1917
War Diary	Vlamertinghe	09/03/1917	10/03/1917
War Diary	St Jean	11/03/1917	13/03/1917
War Diary	St Jean Bellevue	14/03/1918	16/03/1918
War Diary	Wieltje	16/03/1918	16/03/1918
War Diary	Bellevue	17/03/1918	17/03/1918
War Diary	St Jean	17/03/1918	17/03/1918
War Diary	Bellevue	18/03/1918	18/03/1918
War Diary	St Jean Bellevue	19/03/1918	19/03/1918
War Diary	Bellevue	20/03/1918	20/03/1918
War Diary	St Jean	21/03/1918	21/03/1918
War Diary	Bellevue	22/03/1918	22/03/1918
War Diary	St Jean	22/03/1918	22/03/1918
War Diary	Bellevue	23/03/1918	24/03/1918
War Diary	Lamkeet	24/03/1918	24/03/1918
War Diary	St Jean Sheet 28 D13180	26/03/1918	26/03/1918
War Diary	Bellevue	26/03/1918	26/03/1918
War Diary	St Jean	26/03/1918	26/03/1918
War Diary	Passchendaele	26/03/1918	26/03/1918
War Diary	Spree Farm	26/03/1918	26/03/1918
War Diary	St Jean	26/03/1918	26/03/1918
War Diary	Passchendaele	27/03/1918	27/03/1918
War Diary	Bellevue	27/03/1918	27/03/1918
War Diary	St Jean	27/03/1918	27/03/1918
War Diary	Bellevue	28/03/1918	28/03/1918
War Diary	St Jean Sheet 28 D13 F80	29/03/1918	29/03/1918

War Diary	St Jean Sheet 28 D13 F80	30/03/1918	30/03/1918
War Diary	Bellevue	30/03/1918	30/03/1918
War Diary	St Jean Sheet 28 D13 F80	31/03/1918	31/03/1918
War Diary	St Jean	31/03/1918	31/03/1918
War Diary	Bellevue	31/03/1918	31/03/1918
War Diary	St Jean	31/03/1918	31/03/1918
Heading	War Diary Of Y/29 T.M.B. R.A. From March 1st 1918 To March 31st 1918. Volume 20		
War Diary	Poperinghe	01/03/1918	08/03/1918
War Diary	St Jean	08/03/1918	08/03/1918
War Diary	Vlamertinghe	09/03/1918	09/03/1918
War Diary	St Jean	10/03/1918	10/03/1918
War Diary	Vlamertinghe	11/03/1918	11/03/1918
War Diary	St Jean	12/03/1918	12/03/1918
War Diary	Bellevue	12/03/1918	12/03/1918
War Diary	St Jean	13/03/1918	13/03/1918
War Diary	Bellevue	14/03/1918	14/03/1918
War Diary	St Jean	15/03/1918	15/03/1918
War Diary	Valour Farm	15/03/1918	16/03/1918
War Diary	Bellevue	16/03/1918	17/03/1918
War Diary	St Jean	17/03/1918	18/03/1918
War Diary	Bellevue	19/03/1918	19/03/1918
War Diary	St Jean	20/03/1918	20/03/1918
War Diary	Valour Farm	21/03/1918	21/03/1918
War Diary	Bellevue	22/03/1918	22/03/1918
War Diary	Passonendaele	23/03/1918	23/03/1918
War Diary	Bellevue	24/03/1918	25/03/1918
War Diary	Passchendaele	26/03/1918	26/03/1918
War Diary	St Jean	27/03/1918	27/03/1918
War Diary	Sheet 28 D13 B 80	27/03/1918	27/03/1918
War Diary	St Jean	28/03/1918	28/03/1918
War Diary	Passchendaele	30/03/1918	30/03/1918
War Diary	Bellevue	30/03/1918	31/03/1918
Heading	29th Divisional Artillery. X/29 Trench Mortar Battery April 1918.		
Heading	War Diary Of X/29 Trench Mortar Battery R.A. From: April 1st 1918 To April 30th 1918 Volume 21		
War Diary	Bellevue	01/04/1918	02/04/1918
War Diary	St Jean	03/04/1918	04/04/1918
War Diary	Bellevue	05/04/1918	05/04/1918
War Diary	St Jean	06/04/1918	09/04/1918
War Diary	Bellevue	10/04/1918	12/04/1918
War Diary	Vlamertinghe	13/04/1918	26/04/1918
War Diary	Hamhoek	27/04/1918	29/04/1918
Heading	29th Divisional Artillery. Y/29 Trench Mortar Battery April 1918.		
Heading	War Diary Of Y/29 Trench Mortar Battery R.A. From: April 1st 1918 To: April 30th 1918 Volume 21		
War Diary	St Jean	01/04/1918	02/04/1918
War Diary	Bellevue	02/04/1918	02/04/1918
War Diary	St Jean	03/04/1918	05/04/1918
War Diary	Bellevue	05/04/1918	05/04/1918
War Diary	Valour Farm	06/04/1918	06/04/1918
War Diary	St Jean	06/04/1918	07/04/1918
War Diary	Passchendaele	07/04/1918	07/04/1918
War Diary	St Jean	08/04/1918	09/04/1918

War Diary	Bellevue	10/04/1918	10/04/1918
War Diary	St Jean	10/04/1918	10/04/1918
War Diary	Bellevue	11/04/1918	11/04/1918
War Diary	St Jean	12/04/1918	12/04/1918
War Diary	Road Camp	13/04/1918	13/04/1918
War Diary	St Jean	14/04/1918	15/04/1918
War Diary	Dead End	15/04/1918	16/04/1918
War Diary	Road Camp	17/04/1918	17/04/1918
War Diary	Vlamertinge	18/04/1918	21/04/1918
War Diary	Wieltje	22/04/1918	23/04/1918
War Diary	Vlamertinghe	24/04/1918	24/04/1918
War Diary	Wieltje	25/04/1918	25/04/1918
War Diary	Vlamertinghe	25/04/1918	26/04/1918
War Diary	Hamhoek	27/04/1918	30/04/1918
Heading	War Diary Of X/29th Trench Mortar Battery R.A. From May 1st 1918 To May 31st 1918 Volume 22		
War Diary	Hamhoek	01/05/1918	15/05/1918
War Diary	Wallon Cappel	16/05/1918	18/05/1918
War Diary	Sec-Bois	19/10/1918	26/10/1918
War Diary	Wallon Cappele	26/05/1918	30/05/1918
War Diary	Sec Bois	31/05/1918	31/05/1918
Heading	War Diary Of Y/29 Trench Mortar Battery R.A. From May 1st 1918 To May 31st 1918 Volume 22		
War Diary	Hamhoek	01/05/1918	12/05/1918
War Diary	Ypres	12/05/1918	12/05/1918
War Diary	Hamhoek	13/05/1918	13/05/1918
War Diary	Wallon Cappel	14/05/1918	22/05/1918
War Diary	E 27 D 75	23/05/1918	23/05/1918
War Diary	Wallon Cappel	24/05/1918	24/05/1918
War Diary	E16 A 97	25/05/1918	25/05/1918
War Diary	Sec Bois	26/05/1918	30/05/1918
War Diary	E27d75	30/05/1918	31/05/1918
Heading	War Diary Of Y/29th Trench Mortar Battery R.A. From June 1st 1918 To June 30th 1918 Volume 23		
War Diary	Sheet 36A NE	04/06/1918	08/06/1918
War Diary	Sec Bois	01/06/1918	03/06/1918
War Diary	Sec Bois	09/06/1918	12/06/1918
War Diary	Sheet 36 A N.E.	13/06/1918	16/06/1918
War Diary	Sec Bois	17/06/1918	21/06/1918
War Diary	Sheet 36 A N.E	22/06/1918	24/06/1918
War Diary	D15 A 3570	25/06/1918	27/06/1918
War Diary	Sheet 36 A N.E	28/06/1918	30/06/1918
Heading	War Diary Of X/29th Trench Mortar Battery R A From June 1st 1918 To June 30th 1918 Volume 23		
War Diary	Sec Bois	05/06/1918	08/06/1918
War Diary	Sheet 36 A N.E.	01/06/1918	04/06/1918
War Diary	Sheet 36 A N.E	08/06/1918	12/06/1918
War Diary	Sec Bois	13/06/1918	15/06/1918
War Diary	Sheet 36 A N.E	16/06/1918	21/06/1918
War Diary	D15A3570	22/06/1918	24/06/1918
War Diary	Sheet 36 A N.E	25/06/1918	28/06/1918
War Diary	D15A 3570	29/06/1918	30/06/1918
Heading	War Diary Of X/29th Trench Mortar Battery R A From July 1st 1918 To July 31st 1918 Volume 24		
War Diary	Sheet 36 A N.E D15A 3570	01/07/1918	02/07/1918
War Diary	Bandringhem	03/07/1918	22/07/1918

War Diary	Coinperdu	23/07/1918	31/07/1918
Heading	War Diary Of Y/29 Trench Mortar Battery R A From July 1st 1918 To July 31st 1918 Volume 24		
War Diary	E27D E16a And D Sheet 36 A N.E	01/07/1918	03/07/1918
War Diary	Bandringhem	04/07/1918	22/07/1918
War Diary	Coinperdu	23/07/1918	31/07/1918
Heading	War Diary Of X/29th Trench Mortar Battery R A August 1st 1918 To August 31st 1918 Volume 25		
War Diary	Coin Perdu	01/08/1918	01/08/1918
War Diary	Starzeele	02/08/1918	09/08/1918
War Diary	Hondechem	10/08/1918	15/08/1918
War Diary	Strazeele	16/08/1918	24/08/1918
War Diary	Hondeghen	25/08/1918	30/08/1918
War Diary	Pradelles	31/08/1918	31/08/1918
Heading	War Diary Of Y/29th Trench Mortar Battery R A August 1st 1918 To August 31st 1918 Volume 25		
War Diary	Coinperdu	01/08/1918	01/08/1918
War Diary	Hondeghem	02/08/1918	08/08/1918
War Diary	Strazeele	09/08/1918	16/08/1918
War Diary	Hondeghem	17/08/1918	22/08/1918
War Diary	Strazeele	23/08/1918	30/08/1918
War Diary	Outtersteene	31/08/1918	31/08/1918
Heading	War Diary Of X/29th Trench Mortar Battery R A From September 1st 1918 To September 30th 1918 Volume 26		
War Diary	Strazeele	01/09/1918	05/09/1918
War Diary	Baillieul And Steenwerk	09/09/1918	11/09/1918
War Diary	Borre	12/09/1918	14/09/1918
War Diary	Droglandt	15/09/1918	23/09/1918
War Diary	Vlamertinghe	24/09/1918	27/09/1918
War Diary	Ypres	28/09/1918	30/09/1918
Heading	War Diary Of Y/29 Trench Mortar Battery. R.A. From September 1st 1918 To September 30th 1918 Volume 26.		
War Diary	Bailleul And Steen Weuke Sirazeele	01/09/1918	12/09/1918
War Diary	Borre	13/09/1918	13/09/1918
War Diary	Strazeele	14/09/1918	14/09/1918
War Diary	Droglandt	15/09/1918	23/09/1918
War Diary	Vlamertinghe	24/09/1918	26/09/1918
War Diary	Ypres	27/09/1918	30/09/1918
Heading	War Diary of X/29 Trench Mortar Battery R. A. From October 1st 1918 to October 31st 1918. Volume 27.		
War Diary	Glencourse Wood	01/10/1918	10/10/1918
War Diary	Zedeghem	11/10/1918	16/10/1918
War Diary	Barraken	17/10/1918	17/10/1918
War Diary	Heule	19/10/1918	19/10/1918
War Diary	Staceghem	21/10/1918	21/10/1918
War Diary	St Barbe	27/10/1918	29/10/1918
War Diary	Foote	17/10/1918	31/10/1918
Heading	War Diary Of Y/29 Trench Mortar Battery R. A. From October 1st 1918 To October 31st 1918. Volume 27.		
War Diary	Glencorse Wood	01/10/1918	10/10/1918
War Diary	Ledeghem	11/10/1918	16/10/1918
War Diary	Barraken	17/10/1918	17/10/1918
War Diary	Heule	19/10/1918	19/10/1918
War Diary	Staceghem	21/10/1918	21/10/1918

War Diary	St Barre	27/10/1918	29/10/1918
Heading	War Diary Of X/29 Trench Mortar Battery R.A. 1st November 1918 To 30th November 1918. Volume 28.		
War Diary	Roncq	01/11/1918	01/11/1918
War Diary	Tourcoing	03/11/1918	07/11/1918
War Diary	Zoingue	08/11/1918	09/11/1918
War Diary	St Genois	10/11/1918	10/11/1918
War Diary	Sells	13/11/1918	13/11/1918
War Diary	Wobecq	15/11/1918	15/11/1918
War Diary	Marcq	18/11/1918	18/11/1918
War Diary	Saintes Wisherq	21/11/1918	21/11/1918
War Diary	Braine Lalleud	23/11/1918	23/11/1918
War Diary	Chastre	25/11/1918	25/11/1918
War Diary	Grand-Zeez	27/11/1918	27/11/1918
War Diary	Waret-Zeveque	28/11/1918	28/11/1918
War Diary	Stree	29/11/1918	29/11/1918
War Diary	Geromont	30/11/1918	30/11/1918
Heading	War Diary Of Y/29 Trench Mortar Battery R.A. 1st November 1918 to 30th November 1918. Volume 28.		
War Diary	Roncq	01/11/1918	02/11/1918
War Diary	Turcoing	03/11/1918	06/11/1918
War Diary	Dottinghe	07/11/1918	08/11/1918
War Diary	St Genosis	09/11/1918	09/11/1918
War Diary	ARC Banieres	10/11/1918	12/11/1918
War Diary	Wodecq	13/11/1918	17/11/1918
War Diary	Bever	18/11/1918	20/11/1918
War Diary	Steenkup	21/11/1918	22/11/1918
War Diary	Mont St Pont.	23/11/1918	24/11/1918
War Diary	Hevillers	25/11/1918	26/11/1918
War Diary	Sauvenier	27/11/1918	27/11/1918
War Diary	Forville	28/11/1918	28/11/1918
War Diary	Sarte	29/11/1918	29/11/1918
War Diary	Geromont	30/11/1918	30/11/1918
Heading	War Diary X/29 Trench. Mortar Battery December 1918		
War Diary	Geromont	01/12/1918	03/12/1918
War Diary	Remouchamps	04/12/1918	04/12/1918
War Diary	Framcorchamps	05/12/1918	05/12/1918
War Diary	Wiesmes	06/12/1918	06/12/1918
War Diary	Montjie	07/12/1918	07/12/1918
War Diary	Schmidt.	08/10/1918	08/10/1918
War Diary	Muddersheim	09/12/1918	09/12/1918
War Diary	Gelnil	10/12/1918	12/12/1918
War Diary	Berg Gladbach	13/12/1918	31/12/1918
War Diary	Geromont	01/12/1918	03/12/1918
War Diary	Remouchamps	04/12/1918	04/12/1918
War Diary	Framcorchmamps	05/12/1918	05/12/1918
War Diary	Wiesmes	06/12/1918	06/12/1918
War Diary	Montjoie	07/12/1918	07/12/1918
War Diary	Schmidt.	08/12/1918	08/12/1918
War Diary	Muddersheim	09/12/1918	09/12/1918
War Diary	Glenil	10/12/1918	10/12/1918
War Diary	Berg Gladbach	13/12/1918	31/12/1918
Heading	War Diary Y/29 Trench Mortar Battery December		
War Diary	Geromont.	01/12/1918	03/12/1918
War Diary	Aywaille	04/12/1918	04/12/1918

War Diary	Neveze	05/10/1918	05/10/1918
War Diary	Maimedy	05/12/1918	05/12/1918
War Diary	Montjoie	07/12/1918	07/12/1918
War Diary	Rollesbroich	08/12/1918	08/12/1918
War Diary	Zulpich	09/12/1918	09/12/1918
War Diary	Hurth	10/12/1918	12/12/1918
War Diary	Navenhaus	13/12/1918	20/12/1918
War Diary	Berg Gladbach	21/12/1918	31/12/1918
War Diary	Geromont	01/12/1918	03/12/1918
War Diary	Aywaille	04/12/1918	04/12/1918
War Diary	Niveze	05/12/1918	05/12/1918
War Diary	Malmedy.	06/12/1918	06/12/1918
War Diary	Montjie	07/12/1918	07/12/1918
War Diary	Rollesbroich	08/12/1918	08/12/1918
War Diary	Zulpich	09/12/1918	09/12/1918
War Diary	Hurth	10/12/1918	12/12/1918
War Diary	Navenhaus	13/12/1918	20/12/1918
War Diary	Berg Gladbach	21/12/1918	31/12/1918
Heading	Rhine Army Southern Division Late 29th Division 'X' & 'Y' Trench Mortar Btts. Jan 1919		
Heading	War Diary (X/29 T.M.B.) January 1919		
War Diary	Berg Gladbach	01/01/1919	31/01/1919
Heading	War Diary (Y/29 T.M.B). January 1919		
War Diary	Berg Gladbach	01/01/1919	01/01/1919
War Diary	Berg Gladbach	01/01/1919	31/01/1919

WO95/2292/3
Divisional Trench Mortar Batteries

29TH DIVISION TROOPS

TRENCH MORTAR BATTERIES
AUG 1916 – JAN 1919

29th Division

"S" 29 TRENCH MORTAR BATTERY

AUGUST 1 9 1 6

WAR DIARY
or
INTELLIGENCE SUMMARY.
(Erase heading not required.)

Army Form C. 2118.

S.29 Trench Mortar Battery

Place	Date	Hour	Summary of Events and Information	Remarks and references to Appendices
Mailly	1-8-16 to 31-8-16		Tuesday 1st to Sunday 6th nothing of importance to record weather fine & hot & sunny. No rain. General amount of shelling. Fired 40 Rds on Thirst Line 4th inst. Result Sap Head Blown up. Line blown in 1 Rd dropped short in our own wire (Did not explode). Monday 7th Battery brought out of action. Relieved at 4.0pm by x Battery 6th Division. They did not take up position evacuated by S.29 T.M.B, but continued a new position in front line between Marlborough Trench & Seaforth Trench. Wednesday 9th General Parade. Marching order. To proceed to Orville for 10 days rest. Left billet at 2.15pm arrived at Orville 4.0pm. 9th to 16th Battery at rest at Orville weather remained excellent. 10th Trench Battery inspected by General Peake 16th inst orders received to return to Line & take over old position & relieve x 6. T.M.B. Battery in action 6.0 AM 17th inst. Fired 40 Rds Result unobserved. Wednesday 16th No. 66888 Bomb. Archer James Hardy awarded Military "Medal" for distinguished service on for July 1916. 558 Gr. J. Ackerman & 549 Gr. Rees J.A. were admitted into hospital.	Vol-1

WAR DIARY
or
INTELLIGENCE SUMMARY.

Of S.29 Trench Mortar Battery. (Cont.)

18th to 20th Weather fine. Monday 21st Enemy fire blew in two positions & set on fire an adjacent bomb store & broke some two service bombs. G⁰ Buxtin No 1005 WH & Lummis E No 7647.5 put this out by shovelling earth on it after it had burned some 2 hrs drawing Enemy fire on the line & on positions. This act was reported to D.A.H.Q. 22ⁿᵈ to 25th weather changed, slightly becoming colder. Battery busy repairing pits & constructing magazine. Saturday 26th heavy fire from Enemy Trench Mortars in Beaumont Hamel. Replied to with 42 Rds. No apparent damage caused to Mortars, but neighbourhood severely damaged. 27th weather very wet. 28th & 29th weather remained bad, night of 28th 200 Rds ammunition expected did not arrive owing to shortage of transport. 30th to 31st weather slightly improved. 30th Enemy fire very severe on left sections position No 3 Gun position blown in, a gun damaged. Ordnance stores very hard to obtain, during this month owing to divisions changing fronts.

WAR DIARY
or
INTELLIGENCE SUMMARY.

of S.29 Trench Mortar Battery. (cont-d) Army Form C. 2118.

Place	Date	Hour	Summary of Events and Information	Remarks references to Appendices

Rations very satisfactory. Fresh meat supply exceptionally good. Gun stores indented for on June 26th not arrived up to date. This greatly impedes the efficiency of battery. No 4 Gun being out of action owing to lack of spare parts.

Signed J.R.Mann
O.C. S.29 Trench Mortar Battery

29th Division.

&V" 29 HEAVY TRENCH MORTAR BATTERY

AUGUST 1 9 1 6

WAR DIARY or INTELLIGENCE SUMMARY.

(Erase heading not required.)

Army Form C. 2118.

V/29 T.M Battery

Place	Date	Hour	Summary of Events and Information	Remarks and references to Appendices
HAMEL	21/8/16		Owing to death of Capt W. Chapman R.F.A. 2nd Lt W.H. CRAIB placed in command of Battery. Rest of Bty. Battery sent to billets in MAILLY-MAILLET. Informed & reported verbally by T.M.O. 29 R.S.A that no more Trench Mortar Ammunition available, also that no higher than 4th first velocity officers permission from O.C. A/29 R.F.A being obtained for fire on 19.R.	
"	22/8/16		Instructions received from T.M.O. 29 R. 29 R.M. to proceed with Strafe Runs if not against enemy fire. Instructions were Cto shot each 6P.M. in HAMEL for this purpose. Permission granted verbally by Capt. J. R. S. M. to O.C. Bty 4 T.M.B. to fire ammunition if reserves together than 4 am higher for number to be forwarded as forecast & be forwarded ammunition expenditure.	
"	23/8/16		Instructions received from K.T.M.O. 29 R.A to forward complete list of deficiencies of all stores in Battery. This complied with. Also an order to forward dairy ammunition return to this office before 4 pm. Arrangements made with O.C. mounted Section to withdraw men in line of fire of heavy French Mortars in this sector. 6 rounds fired from English gun on point Q.30.50.52 5pm offer strafe ordered. Trenches in neighbourhood of	All m.b coordinates refer to map 57 S.E 1&2

WAR DIARY
or
INTELLIGENCE SUMMARY.

(Erase heading not required.)

Army Form C. 2118.

Place	Date	Hour	Summary of Events and Information	Remarks and references to Appendices
HAMEL	23/3/16	9.30pm	10 pltps/os 40'x 9" dim. plus 1500 sandbags arrived from R.E.O. Indent for 1000' of Elephant wire sent in. (to try him to near O.P.)	
	2/4/16	9 am	All men employed in deepening trenches round Junction, and constructing firesteps for steel loopholes.	
		Noon	Inspection of Latrines by MEDICAL OFFICER	
			Men & NCO Rogers moved from R.A.O. to give 6 men as working party to help complete construction of 2 new pits in HAMEL. The O.C. supplied with working party made on instructions of S.B. Day & night & Subaltern same.	
		7.30pm	30 rds English Amm'n arrives at dump. Were carried up to F.L.	
			O/C I/ORO received from Bg 44 H.Q. that 14 rounds big Am'n to be expend at dump at 7.30pm Also to watch expenditure of Am'n so much as possible and to furnish a report of all rounds fired, target &c. to Division Officer at Battalion Hdqrs at 9 am daily.	

WAR DIARY
or
INTELLIGENCE SUMMARY.
(Erase heading not required.)

Army Form C. 2118.

Instructions regarding War Diaries and Intelligence Summaries are contained in F.S. Regs., Part II. and the Staff Manual respectively. Title pages will be prepared in manuscript.

Place	Date	Hour	Summary of Events and Information	Remarks and references to Appendices
HAMEL	25/4/16	11 am	All gas helmets inspected. Indent for helmets to replace faulty helmets and deficiencies sent in.	
		4 pm	Draft of 14 men arrive from R.A.C. to bring Battery to Full Strength. 1 man sent with Chest trouble. Not notified to authorities concerned.	
		5-6 pm	5 rounds fired on French (enemy) Tramway below bank parallel to railway at point Q.16.c.20.60. 10k'd round. (2-x short). First shot. Shot in channel British Trenches at Q.10.c.30.05. Short, one is faulty round.	
		10 pm 11 pm	Battery Drays (Rabinsky's Bays) took ?	
	26/4/	9 am	Took in Trench round position and fur ties) had been summed. Horse H..A..morning at dump Carriage.	
		6 pm	Brass C instructions returned to Battal in NAPLEY-en-MESNIL A-C subsection take their place in Action at guns.	
		8 pm 11 pm	W..K. instructed on New M.P.T's. 2nd Lt. J. P. Bowman R.F.A. posted to V/29 H.T.M.B. from B.H.E.	

T2131. Wt. W708-776. 500000. 4/15. Sir J. C. & S.

Army Form C. 2118.

WAR DIARY
or
INTELLIGENCE SUMMARY.
(Erase heading not required.)

Instructions regarding War Diaries and Intelligence Summaries are contained in F. S. Regs., Part II. and the Staff Manual respectively. Title pages will be prepared in manuscript.

Place	Date	Hour	Summary of Events and Information	Remarks and references to Appendices
HAMEL	2/7/16	noon	Change from 2nd Wgt.RA orders us to continue rate of rapid rate as now. Rts. also that higher form to be cut down and mounted. Report received from 1810 specials to come rest on New Pt. but to place between guns on [illegible].	
			Weather changing — showers of rain at intervals. Atmosphere close becoming very sultry.	
			Trench mortars at Camp 9 have brought up to join Pt's to do places on French Gott.	
	28/9/16	9am	English fire placed on French front in No.1 Pt.	
		9am	Body of 2 guns later up and went ahead with new timber.	
		3pm	2 rifle Big Arm Bought up. 2 men slightly burned Gunsmithy heart for preventions.	
			Weather, continue showery throughout. Report of heavy losses	

T2131. Wt. W708-776. 500000. 4/16. Sir J. C. & S.

WAR DIARY

SUMMARY OF EVENTS AND INFORMATION

Place	Date	Hour	Summary of Events & Information	Remarks
HAMEL	29/8/16	11.30am to 12 noon	9 Rounds fired, 4 from No.1 gun, 5 from No.2 gun, to test working of Snghot piece on Trench Cradle, and to test new bed for No.2 gun laid on 28/8/16. Both guns fired excellently. No damage to No.1 gun or Cradle - no damage. Probably one infantry charge. Target - enemy trenches in Q.18.C.	
		9.30pm	30 rounds sent up and embodied in steam HAMEL owing to intense darkness & rain impossible to carry same up to position. Trenches in bad condition.	
			Raining practically all day.	
	30/8/16	9am	20 rounds brought up from dump.	
		5pm	A and C Subsections from billet replace B and D subsections at guns. Telephone wire run out to O.P. at Jacobs Ladder.	

W.H. Grant Capt.
O.C. 1/5 H.T.M.B.

29th Division.

"Z" 29 TRENCH MORTAR BATTERY

AUGUST 1 9 1 6

Army Form C. 2118.

9/29 Wentworth Ruler

WAR DIARY
or
INTELLIGENCE SUMMARY.
(Erase heading not required.)

Instructions regarding War Diaries and Intelligence Summaries are contained in F. S. Regs., Part II. and the Staff Manual respectively. Title pages will be prepared in manuscript.

Place	Date	Hour	Summary of Events and Information	Remarks and references to Appendices
BEAUMONT	1.8.16		The battery kept three guns in action firing desultorily cutting wire & retaliating on enemy trenches as occasion arose. It was noticed that immediately we fired two or three rounds the enemy would cease firing the heavy minenwerfer which used to cause particular annoyance.	
HAMEL Sector	2.8.16			
SOMME	3.8.16			
"	4.8.16			
AMPLIER	5.8.16		The battery left the line & proceeded by lorries to AMPLIER, PAS DE CALAIS	
PAS de CALAIS	15.8.16		The battery remained here until 15.8.16 resting & refitting	
"	15.8.16		The battery proceeded back to the line taking over on the night of the 15.8.16 our previous position from 2/Guards T.M.B. that had relieved them on the 5.8.16	
BEAUMONT	16.8.16		Desultory firing mostly in retaliation against enemy minenwerfers	
HAMEL Sector	17.8.16		do	
	18.8.16	16.30 & 19.45	Two dummy raids were carried out by the 9th Batt. Norfolks. We cooperated with the Artillery according to programme firing on the enemy front line trenches at Q.10.d.55.80 Map 57d S.E.	
	19.8.16	12.00	A British aeroplane flying very low on account of the mist was being harassed by enemy rifle & machine gun fire. 6 rounds were immediately fired into the enemy trenches & the firing was not heard again	

T2134. Wt. W708-776. 50000. 4/15. Sir J. C. & S.

WAR DIARY
or
INTELLIGENCE SUMMARY.
(Erase heading not required.)

Army Form C. 2118.

Instructions regarding War Diaries and Intelligence Summaries are contained in F. S. Regs., Part II. and the Staff Manual respectively. Title pages will be prepared in manuscript.

Place	Date	Hour	Summary of Events and Information	Remarks and references to Appendices
BEAUMONT	20.8.16		A few rounds fired in retaliation with excellent effect.	
HAMEL Sector	21.8.16		A raid was made by the 9th Batt. Suffolks at Q.10.d Map 57 d. S.E. the battery did not participate.	
	22.8.16		About 25 rounds were fired at the wire Q.10.d.55.60 – Q.10.d.55.80 with good effect. An arrangement was made with the sector M.G. Coy to spray the wire at intervals during the night. As the infantry sent out patrols which were sometimes away four hours at a stretch it was impossible to fire and the enemy repaired his wire every time.	
	23.8.16		59 rounds were fired with same effect & effect as on 22.8.16. At 20.00 – 20.30 the enemy retaliated heavily on the whole sector front. A fair amount of damage was done to the trenches in the region of the gun pits.	
	24.8.16		No firing during the day. 4 rounds retaliation in evening.	
	25.8.16		80 rounds fired at wire cutting several broad lanes at "Spur" Q.10.d.	
	26.8.16		No firing took place.	
	27.8.16 1.00		20 rounds were fired on wire which had been partly repaired during the night.	
	28.8.16 13.30		10 rounds fired on wire Q.10.d.55.60.	

Army Form C. 2118.

WAR DIARY
or
INTELLIGENCE SUMMARY.
(Erase heading not required.)

Instructions regarding War Diaries and Intelligence Summaries are contained in F. S. Regs., Part II. and the Staff Manual respectively. Title pages will be prepared in manuscript.

Place	Date	Hour	Summary of Events and Information	Remarks and references to Appendices
BEAUMONT	29.8.16		10 rounds fired on wire O.10.d.55.70. No retaliation was required.	
HAMEL Sector	30.8.16	1400	10 rounds were fired to-day at wire O.10.d with good results. No retaliation has been required during the last 24 hours.	J.C. 2/29 T.M.B.

T/134. Wt. W708-776. 500000. 4/15. Sir J. C. & S.

29th Division.

"V" 29 HEAVY TRENCH MORTAR BATTERY

SEPTEMBER 1 9 1 6

— CONFIDENTIAL —

WAR DIARY

OF

V29 H.T.M.B.

FROM 1·9·16   TO 29·9·16

VOLUME N°

Army Form C. 2118.

WAR DIARY
or
INTELLIGENCE SUMMARY.
(Erase heading not required.)

Place	Date	Hour	Summary of Events and Information	Remarks and references to Appendices
HAMEL	1/9/16		Requests by O.C. Infantry Bde Battn Hdqrs to discontinue firing till advised by him, so as to avoid being retaliation on trenches in neighbourhood of pits. This reported to D.T.M.O. 29 Bde asking for advice on matter.	
"		11 a.m.	Gas Helmet inspection - all men deficient of Helmets supplied. Transfer of Gr. Thompson (No. 29275) to O. 168 Bde R.F.A. arranged. 30 rds. AMMUN. arrived.	
"	2/9/16		Order received from D.T.M.O. to evacuate pits, leaving guard of 3 men at 6 p.m. Complied with.	
MAILLY-MAILLET	3/9/16		Orders from D.T.M.O. to Bayonet complete Clothing & Equipment deficiencies in Battery. Complied with. Sky overcast - prospect of rain.	
"	4/9/16		Reported by N.C.O. from HAMEL that F. Fatigue Parties since 10 a.m. 3/9/16. D.T.M.O. notified. Search made without success. Sky overcast - much rain.	
"	5/9/16		Handed over guns telephone line, ammunition & pits to O.C. V 39 H.T.M.B. guards from Pits in HAMEL and WHITE CITY withdrawn. Intermittent showers of rain.	
"	6/9/16		Orders from D.T.M.O. to Prepare to leave billets in MAILLY on 7/9/16 - Battery to proceed to. Handed over guns & Stores to O.C. V 39 H.T.M.B.	

Army Form C. 2118

WAR DIARY or INTELLIGENCE SUMMARY

(Erase heading not required.)

Instructions regarding War Diaries and Intelligence Summaries are contained in F.S. Regs., Part II. and the Staff Manual respectively. Title Pages will be prepared in manuscript.

Place	Date	Hour	Summary of Events and Information	Remarks and references to Appendices
MAILLY-MAILLET	6/9/16		Transfer of Sgt. Hammond to 146 Siege Battery. R.G.A. Battery resting.	
"	7/9/16		Battery moved to Louvencourt – personnel only. Pay issued to Battery.	
"	8/9/16		Battery at rest in billets in Louvencourt.	
"	9/9/16		1 N.C.O. placed under arrest by M.M.P. Battery at rest.	
Louvencourt	10/9/16		Battery entrained at Belle Eglise Station for new sector. (YPRES SALIENT)	
Field	11/9/16		Spent 18 hours at Romescamp Siding. Enroute for Poperinghe via Abbeville & Calais.	
Poperinghe	12/9/16		Arrived at Poperinghe. New billets in "Hut outside town of POPERINGHE".	
"	13/9/16		2 NCOs & 18 men warned by T.M.O. to be ready to proceed to T.M. School at BERTHEN on 16th 19/16. 10 H.T.M. Battle slings issued to be reported on after use.	
"	14/9/16		Battery entrained POPERINGHE	
"	15/9/16		Equipment & stores &c for 10 helmets, periscopes, blankets, steel helmets, field books forwarded to T.M.O. Also statement re no.1 N.C.O's & men who have not had leave for 12 months. Return of natural forms for group Pts. forwarded.	
YPRES	16/9/16		Battery moved from Poperinghe to Billets in YPRES. 2 NCO's & 24 men attached to T.M. School New Pit mustered. Fatigue parties provided to help in construction.	
"	17/9/16		Took over 1 H.T.M. mortar from O.C. V/4 H.T.M.B. Fatigue parties working day & night at 1 Telephone attached to artillery by under 6 T.M.O's staff. Fatigue on pit.	
"	18/9/16		Introduced to the Telephone wire fatigues provides for pit construction.	
"	19/9/16		Statement re no. of trained men T.M.O.'s in Battery forwarded to T.M.O.	
"	20/9/16			

Army Form C. 2118

WAR DIARY
or
INTELLIGENCE SUMMARY

(Erase heading not required.)

Instructions regarding War Diaries and Intelligence Summaries are contained in F. S. Regs., Part II. and the Staff Manual respectively. Title Pages will be prepared in manuscript.

Place	Date	Hour	Summary of Events and Information	Remarks and references to Appendices
YPRES.	20/9/16		2 Claims (shrared) (n. H.T.M.) made by R.E's. Fatigues busy at Pit.	
	21/9/16		Position for 2nd H.T.Mortar reconnoitred — probably in Railway Wood at I.N.6.50.20. (Sheet 25) S².T.6.a.1.n.	
	22/9/16		H.T. Howitzes received from H.Q.A.T.S. (4 guns)	
	23/9/16		Work on Pits continued.	
	24/9/16		Fatigues night & day parades for construction of Pit under Progress.	
	25/9/16		Fatigues on pit. Rations not satisfactory. Position (proposed) in Railway Wood condemned by Inspector by C.O.	
	26/9/16		Fatigues.	
	27/9/16		Fatigues ampte. Officers & O.R.'s attached for T.M. Course at Volcot. 2nd New Pattern Box Respirator to men.	
	28/9/16		Fatigues as usual. Pay issued to battery.	
	29/9/16		Orders to put 2 Vickers Guns into Warwick Farm to fire on use of 29th. Fatigue all night. Position in Warwick Farm improved. Gunfire as Mill-Cots nearby (n bed).	

2449 Wt. W14957/M90 750,000 1/16 J.B.C. & A. Forms/C.2118/12.

Casualties

To accompany A.F. B.2118 ...

Date	Officers	O.R's	Remarks
3-9-16		1	Rejoined from Hospl
-"-		1	Missing from casualties
5-9-16		1	Admitted to Hospital (sick)
9-9-16		1	Returned to former Bty
-"-		2	Admitted to Hospital (sick)
10-9-16		2	Admitted to Hospital (injured)
13-9-16		1	Admitted to Hospital (sick)
13-9-16		1	-"-
-"-		1	Rejoined from Hospital
-"-		1	Returned to former Bty
17-9-16		16	Attached to 4th Army T.M. School for instructions
-"-		1	Admitted to Hospital (sick)
20-9-16		1	Attached to Y Bty T.M.
-"-		1	Admitted to Hospital (sick)
20-9-16		2	-"- -"- -"-
27-9-16		1	Rejoined from Trench Train
29-9-16		1	-"- from Hospital

D.H. Craib Lieut R.F.A.
Comdg V.29 H.T.M.B.

29th Division.

"X" 29 TRENCH MORTAR BATTERY

SEPTEMBER 1 9 1 6

— CONFIDENTIAL —

WAR DIARY
OF
X/29 T.M.B

FROM 1-9-16 TO 30/9/16

VOLUME N° 2

Army Form C. 2118.

WAR DIARY
or
INTELLIGENCE SUMMARY.
(Erase heading not required.)

X 29 TMB

Instructions regarding War Diaries and Intelligence Summaries are contained in F. S. Regs., Part II. and the Staff Manual respectively. Title pages will be prepared in manuscript.

Place	Date	Hour	Summary of Events and Information	Remarks and references to Appendices
HAMEL	1 Sep		Battery in action at usual spot Shells on MARTINSART WOOD	Annexe
			Fired 60 rounds in answer in front of Jerman trenches	Annexe
			Map Reference BEAUMONT Q 18 d 50·50 Ofr in Roberts trench	Annexe
	2		Fired 50 rounds Same objective	Annexe
		6pm	with draw all batt. to MARTINSART except 2 sections on front	Annexe
MARTINSART	3		Remained in billets at MARTINSART	Annexe
	4		do do	Annexe
	5	7pm	Handed over pits to X batt. 39th Division	Annexe
	6	2am	Removed all material from HAMEL & MARTINSART	Annexe
	"		Remained at MARTINSART	Annexe
		11am	Village shelled with heavy shells	Annexe
	7	8am	Left MARTINSART & took entire Battery with equipment to LOUVENCOURT	
			2 fit waggons to LOUVENCOURT	
	8		The inspection at LOUVENCOURT Overhauling limbers	Annexe

T2134. Wt. W708—776. 500000. 4/15. Sir J. C. & 8.

Army Form C. 2118.

WAR DIARY
or
INTELLIGENCE SUMMARY.
(Erase heading not required.)

Instructions regarding War Diaries and Intelligence Summaries are contained in F. S. Regs., Part II. and the Staff Manual respectively. Title pages will be prepared in manuscript.

Place	Date	Hour	Summary of Events and Information	Remarks and references to Appendices
LICOURTENCOURT	Apr 9	10 AM	Bathing Parade	Amd
do	10	11 AM	Church Parade	Amd
BELLE EGLISE	10	4 pm	Entrained at Antheux for POPERINGHE	Amd
	11		In train	Amd
POPERINGHE	12	9 pm	Arrived	Amd
do	13		Now on little embarking find	Amd
do	14	10 pm	Other inspects pits of 4th gun Artillery in the YPRES Salient before taking over	Amd
do	15		Awaiting orders	Amd
Ypres	16		Marched to billets in Ypres	Amd
	17		Making & improving emplacements in the Left Sect.	Amd
	18		do	Amd
	19		do	Amd
	20		do	Amd
	21		do	Amd
	22		do 2/Lt G.F. Sadler R.F.A. leaves the Battery	Amd

T2134. Wt. W708—776. 500000. 4/15. Sir J. C. & S.

Army Form C. 2118.

WAR DIARY
or
INTELLIGENCE SUMMARY.
(Erase heading not required.)

X.29. T.M.B.

Instructions regarding War Diaries and Intelligence Summaries are contained in F.S. Regs., Part II. and the Staff Manual respectively. Title pages will be prepared in manuscript.

Place	Date	Hour	Summary of Events and Information	Remarks and references to Appendices
Ypres	1916 Sept. 23		Improving emplacements & constructing new ones.	Annex.
"	24		do	Annex.
"	25		do	Annex.
"	26		do	Annex.
"	27		Putting in guns at S.O. Support line (Minnies) o/o John Street.	Annex.
"	28		do	Annex.
"	29		do	Annex.
"	30		do	Annex.

29th Division.

"Y" 29 TRENCH MORTAR BATTERY

SEPTEMBER 1 9 1 6

— CONFIDENTIAL —

WAR DIARY

OF

Y/29 T.M.B

FROM 24-9-16 TO 30/9/16

VOLUME N° 2

WAR DIARY
or
INTELLIGENCE SUMMARY.
(Erase heading not required.)

Army Form C. 2118.

Place	Date	Hour	Summary of Events and Information	Remarks and references to Appendices
Ypres.	24/8/15		Lt Wylie evacuated to Hospital. Battery taken over by Lt Provos.	L.v.H.T.
	25"		Preparing Gun Pits	
	26"		Preparing Gun Pits, new gun emplacement commenced.	L.v.H.T.
	27"		Preparing Gun Pits.	L.v.H.T.
	28"		Guns registered on C.29.A.30.9.5. from 18.30 P.m. till 19.00.	L.v.H.T.
	29"		Guns re registered on C.29.A.30.9.5. from 12 till 12.45. German Bomb store in the enemy front line trench blown up by No.3 gun. Enemy replied with Minen Warfer during the night, but failed to do any material damage.	L.v.H.T.
	30		Preparations made for supporting the raid at night.	L.v.H.T.

L.v.H.Provos.
Lieut. R.F.A.

o/c Y/29/F.M.B.

29th Division

"Z" 29 TRENCH MORTAR BATTERY

"A
SEPTEMBER 1 9 1 6

CONFIDENTIAL

WAR DIARY

OF

Z/29 T.M.B

FROM 1-9-16 TO 30/9/16

WAR DIARY or INTELLIGENCE SUMMARY

Army Form C. 2118.

J 29 Trench Mortar Battery

Place	Date	Hour	Summary of Events and Information	Remarks and references to Appendices
In The Field.	3.9.16		A joint bombardment on trenches in front of Beaumont Hamel, attack made further south which was not successful.	
	6.9.16		Reinforcements arrived from "S" 29 Trench Mortar Battery which consisted of Lt Graham L.E.V. 2/Lt Shaw V.C. and 12 men, Lt Graham taking over 7/c. 2/Lt Chadwick 2/Lt Corbett and 20 men transferred to 29th D.A.C.	
	7.9.16		We departed from Mailly Maillet for North, staying at Lovencourt 3 days, leaving on the 12th, staying at Poperinghe for 3 days when we entrained arriving at Poperinghe on the 13th, staying at Poperinghe for 3 days, when we departed for Ypres arriving at Ypres on the 15th, to take over positions from the 11th Division. On taking over we were given 10 days to strengthen them, which were in a very bad condition.	
	21.9.16		Lt Graham and 2 men transferred to the 4th Division, 2/Lt Shaw V.C. taking over 7/c of the battery, 2/Lt East G.D. joined the battery.	
	27.9.16		Hostile Balloon brought down by our aeroplanes on our right, balloon fell to the ground in flames at 17.50.	

V. Shaw 2/Lt
O/C 2.9 T.M.B.

29th Division.

"V" 29 HEAVY TRENCH MORTAR BATTERY

OCTOBER 1 9 1 6

Vol 2

CONFIDENTIAL

WAR DIARY

of

V/29 H.T.H.B.

from 1st October 1916 to 30th October 1916.

(Volume 2)

W.H.Traill 2nd Lt RFA
O.C. V/29 H.T.H.B.

Army Form C. 2118.

WAR DIARY
or
INTELLIGENCE SUMMARY

(Erase heading not required.)

Instructions regarding War Diaries and Intelligence Summaries are contained in F. S. Regs., Part II. and the Staff Manual respectively. Title Pages will be prepared in manuscript.

Place	Date	Hour	Summary of Events and Information	Remarks and references to Appendices
YPRES	1.10.16		Fatigue party on Gun Pit at Mtl. Cots.	WPC
	2 & 3/10/16		Bad element ready for further. Overhead Cover being improved	WPC
				WPC
	4/10		Gun & Bed down. Overhead Cover + Lung Tunes. Ready for action	
	5/10		Started receiving T.M.O. Gun not to be fired owing to proximity of NEW COTS O.P. so as to avoid detection by artillery of enemy retaliation	WPC
	6 & 7/10		Fatigue Parties each night to complete work on Pit.	WPC
	8/10		Orders received to hand over roll Gun & Ammunition to OC V55-47W63	WPC
	9/10		Battery moves to POPERINGHE (by rail & motor lorry.)	WPC
	10/10		Billets in PROVEN - Pay & c.	WPC
	11/10 4p		Fatigues supplying for entrainment of howrs. 1 & 4 1) from R Battery entrained for PALEAUX on horse PROVEN - VECQUEMONT	WPC
	12 & 13/10		Arrive PALEAUX. Removed by Lorry to Billets in VECQUEMONT.	WPC
	14/10		Billets in VECQUEMONT.	
S22C	15/10		Battery marches to Hp' Camps - Huts available - 2 Kilometres L. ALBERT Battery moves headquarters to gd H.Q. position between MONTAUBAN and LONGUEVAL.	WPC
S22C7070	16/10	10h aon	32 OR attacked to 91st D.A.C. arrv. Druny	

2449 Wt. W14957/M90 750,000 1/16 J.B.C. & A. Forms/C.2118/12.

Army Form C. 2118.

WAR DIARY
or
INTELLIGENCE SUMMARY
(Erase heading not required.)

Instructions regarding War Diaries and Intelligence Summaries are contained in F.S. Regs., Part II. and the Staff Manual respectively. Title Pages will be prepared in manuscript.

Place	Date	Hour	Summary of Events and Information	Remarks and references to Appendices
S.22 C.70.70	17.10.16		Duty on dump (Contains tell 22nd)	60 W.C.
			Newdump formed at Raieleau. (4/15/27.C. Dump) Battery moved to New Dump	47 H.C.
	23.10.16			65 H.C.
	24.10.16		1 Officer 14 O.R.'s attached to 72½ Div. Ammunition Dump	
	27.10.16		Sheepskin jackets issued to Battery.	65 H.C.
	28-30/10/16		On duty at Dumps.	
			(Casualties as per attached)	

T/29 H.T.H. Battery

Casualty List accompanying A.F.C.& 2118 War Diary

Regtl No.	Rk	Name	Nature of Casualty	Remarks
37	Gr	Cottrell H	Joined Bty from 29th D.A.C 30/9/16	
122174	"	Pollard H		
72425	"	Evans T		
76475	"	Cummings E.		
111546	"	Gray W		
61449	"	Quinn G.		
67225	"	Dean R.H		
3363	"	Hopkins F		
68386	"	Wilson JS		
81155	"	Bryant P.		
43488	Bpl	Offer H.	Admitted to hospital Sick 23-9-16	
3319	Gr	Rowley W	Admitted to hospital Sick 30-9-16	
76475	"	Cummings E	Admitted to hospital Sick 30-9-16	
117	"	Janes W.G.	Admitted to hospital Sick 1-10-16	
76475	"	Cummings E	Rejoined from hospl. 2-10-16	
27542	Bpl	Morris S.	Admitted to hospl Sick 4-10-16	
3319	Gr	Rowley W	Rejoined from ho- 6-10-16	
27542	Bpl	Morris S.	Rejoined from hosptl 9-10-16	
22957	Gr	Clarke J	Admitted to hos Sick 17-10-16	
3363	"	Hopkins F.		
122174		Pollard H	Admitted to hos Sick 19-10-16	
100864	Fitter Gr	Barratt A.T	Joined from 29th DAC 21-10-1916	
122174	Gr	Pollard H	Rejoined from hos 23-10-16	
49666	"	Reynolds H	Rejoined from Y Bty TMB. 27-10-16	
22957	"	Clarke J	Rejoined from hos 29-10-16	

31/10/16

O.C. T/29 Heavy Trench Howitzer Bty

29th Division.

"X" 29 TRENCH MORTAR BATTERY

OCTOBER 1 9 1 6

Confidential

War Diary

of

X/29th Trench Mortar Battery R.A.

From 1st October 1916
to 31st October 1916

Volume 3.

Army Form C. 2118.

WAR DIARY
or
INTELLIGENCE SUMMARY.
(Erase heading not required.) X 29 T.M.B

October.

Instructions regarding War Diaries and Intelligence Summaries are contained in F.S. Regs., Part II. and the Staff Manual respectively. Title pages will be prepared in manuscript.

Place	Date	Hour	Summary of Events and Information	Remarks and references to Appendices
	1916			
YPRES	30/9	A 20.30	1 Section opens fire on enemy wire at C.29.a.30.95 from a position in old support line at S.9. After firing 15 rounds the section retired the two guns being but of action. No casualties.	Annied
"	1/10	20:20	In billets at Ypres	Annied
"	2/10		do	Annied
"	3/10		do	Annied
"	4		do	Annied
"	5		do	Annied
"	6		do	Annied
ESQUELBECQ.	7	9 pm	Transport mother lorries & personnel & guns & stores to ESQUELBECQ in billets there.	Annied
"	8	9 pm	Entrained " " " for LONGUEAU at 9. p.m.	Annied
"	9	8 am	Arrived LONGUEAU leaving guns there temporary. Batt. march to DAOURS.	Annied
DAOURS.	10		In billets.	Annied
"	11		do	Annied
CAMP "A"	12		Personnel Guns & stores by motor lorries transport to Camp A. QUERRIER-ALBERT road.	Annied
"	13		Personnel proceed to 5.15.c.3.5 bivouac for the night. Attacked to D.A.C as 1 Section (extra).	Annied
"	14		do	Annied
"	15		Lt. C.V.H. Parsons joined the battery.	Annied
"	16		Improving shelters & making new ones in the open. do	Annied

Army Form C. 2118.

WAR DIARY
or
INTELLIGENCE SUMMARY.
(Erase heading not required.)

X 29 T.M.B.

October '16.

Place	Date	Hour	Summary of Events and Information	Remarks and references to Appendices
	Oct 16			
BAZENTIN	17		In 29th D.A.C. Camp at 5.15.c.3.5 near BAZENTIN-LE-GRAND	—
"	18		Do	—
"	19		Do	—
"	20		Personnel on fatigues for the D.A.C.	—
"	21		Do	—
"	22		Do	—
"	23		Do	—
"	24		Do (Sheet 57c S.W.)	—
"	25	2:30 pm	Battery went into action at N.26.a.15.85. Operations on enemy wire on "Bayonet Trench."	—
"	26		Do	—
"	27		Personnel of Battery returned to camp of 29th D.A.C. at BAZENTIN-LE-GRAND (5.15.c.3.5.) 57c S.W.	—
"	28		At — in camp at Do	—
"	29		" " "	—
"	30		" " "	—
ALBERT.	31	5:00 pm	The Battery personnel guns & stores took motor lorries to billets in ALBERT.	—

29th Division.

"Y" 29 TRENCH MORTAR BATTERY

OCTOBER 1 9 1 6

Vol 3

Confidential

War Diary

of

Y/29th Trench Mortar Battery R.a.

From 1st October 1916
to 31st October 1916

Volume 3.

Army Form C. 2118.

WAR DIARY
or
INTELLIGENCE SUMMARY.
(Erase heading not required.)

Instructions regarding War Diaries and Intelligence Summaries are contained in F.S. Regs., Part II. and the Staff Manual respectively. Title pages will be prepared in manuscript.

Place	Date	Hour	Summary of Events and Information	Remarks and references to Appendices
YPRES	30/9/16	2030	All guns opened fire on C.29.ac.30.95. and continued firing until 2045 when I ordered No 1. and No 2. guns to cease fireing. At 2045 I switched off onto target 20° left of previous target with No 3 & No 4 gun in order to form a barrage on this part of the enemy's trench. After one round on new target No 4 gun was put out of action owing to bed nawing and I continued the barrage with No 3 gun only, until I had expended all ammunition. Retaliation from enemy guns was extremely severe, our front line trench being very heavily bombarded. Ammunition expended on c.29.ac 30.9.5 = 40 rounds. Ammunition expended on barrage = 9 rounds.	G. Nicholson Lieut. R.F.A.
			Slight repairs & alterations made to gun pits	G. Nicholson Lieut. R.F.A.
	1/10/16		General fatigues	S. Nicholson Lieut. R.F.A.
	2/10/16		Ammunition dug out & built	S. Nicholson Lieut. R.F.A.
	3/10/16		Detachments left for trenches a.m.	
	4/10/16			
	5/10/16		Detachments up at Gun Pits for retaliation. Mr Parsons admitted to Hospital.	
	6/10/16		Detachments up at Gun Pits until 1730. relieved by X Battery	
	7/10/16		Cleaning up the guns & stores etc ready for handing over to 5.5.Division.	

WAR DIARY
or
INTELLIGENCE SUMMARY.
(Erase heading not required.)

Army Form C. 2118.

Instructions regarding War Diaries and Intelligence Summaries are contained in F. S. Regs., Part II. and the Staff Manual respectively. Title pages will be prepared in manuscript.

Place	Date	Hour	Summary of Events and Information	Remarks and references to Appendices
YPRES	8-10-16		Lt Moyle reported and took over command. Left YPRES on the right of Oct B/q for ESQUEBEC	A.L.Moyle RFA
ESQUEBEC	9-10-16		In billets	A.Loyle RFA
	10-10-16		Helped to entrain D.A.C. and left at 9 p.m. on train for LONGEAU	A.Loyle RFA
DOUARS	11-10-16		Train LONGEAU about 4 a.m. and marched to DOUARS	A.Loyle RFA
	12-10-16		In billet	
ALBERT	13-10-16		Marched to camp at ALBERT	
CAMP	14-10-16		Marched to camp near MONTAUBAN with D.A.C.	
"	15-10-16		Making shelters for men.	
12 Div. DUMP	16-10-16		Proceeded to 12th Div. Ammunition Dump.	
"	17-10-16		Loading & unloading ammunition	
"	18-10-16		Preparing new dump.	
"	19-10-16		"	
"	20-10-16 — 22-10-16		"	
FLERS	23-10-16		Relieved 2/29 T.M.B. on line near FLERS.	A.L.Moyle Lt RFA O/C Y/24 T.M.B.

T2184. Wt. W708—776. 500000. 4/15. Sir J.C. & S.

WAR DIARY
or
INTELLIGENCE SUMMARY.
(*Erase heading not required.*)

Army Form C. 2118.

Place	Date	Hour	Summary of Events and Information	Remarks and references to Appendices
	Oct 1916			
FLERS	24	0700	Opened fire on enemy line at N.20.c.1-4. 74 rounds fired. Enemy retaliation heavy but ill directed. 2/Lt Ritchie admitted to hospital sick	
"	25		Carried up ammunition. Received orders not to fire any more until further ordrs. 160 relieved by X/29 T.M.B.	
Camps.15.a	26		In dug-outs at camp.	
"	27		In Camp. Lt Wylie returned to duty with 2/29 T.M.B.	
"	28		Battery in camp. General fatigues.	
FLERS	29		Relieved 2/29 in front line. Lt Wylie took over command again.	
"	30		Relieved by 2/1 AUSTRALIAN T.M.B.	
ALBERT	31		Battery proceeded to billets at ALBERT	

A. L. Wylie Lt RFA
o/c X/29 T.M.B.

29th Division.

"Z" 29 TRENCH MORTAR BATTERY

OCTOBER 1 9 1 6

Vol 2

Confidential

War Diary

of

Z/29th Trench Mortar Batteries, R.A.

from 1st October 1916
to 31st October 1916

Volume 3.

1-11-16.

Confidential.

War Diary.
of
Z 29 Trench Mortar Battery

From 1st Oct to 31st 16.

(Volume)

JH Bailey

Army Form C. 2118.

WAR DIARY or INTELLIGENCE SUMMARY

Z.29 Trench Mortar Battery.

(Erase heading not required.)

Instructions regarding War Diaries and Intelligence Summaries are contained in F.S. Regs., Part II. and the Staff Manual respectively. Title Pages will be prepared in manuscript.

Place	Date	Hour	Summary of Events and Information	Remarks and references to Appendices
In the Field.	1-10-16		2nd Lt Eask with 4 men proceeded to the 4th Army T.M. School on a course of instructions. Strafe started at 8.0pm, battery fired 76 Rds.	
		3.00	2nd Lt Salting E.T. transferred from 26TH Battery to Z29 T.M.B	
		3.00 to 7.00	Nothing of importance to report.	
	8TH		The battery left of pent for Esquillee.	
	9TH		At Esquillee.	
	10TH		Helped with entraining D.A.C and left with ½ No. 1 Section at about 6.0pm by No. 19 Train.	
	11TH		Arrived at Longuea about 11.0am and marched to Peguemont. 2nd Lt Shaw V.C admitted to Hospital, 2nd Lt Salting E.T. taking over.	
	12TH			
	13TH		Marched to camp at Albert, remained with D.A.C for the night	
	14TH		Marched to S.I.C. with the D.A.C.	
	15TH		Preparing dug outs for men.	
	16TH		2nd Lt East G.S rejoined the battery from 4th Army T.M. School	
	16TH to 19TH		Nothing of importance	
	20TH		Proceeded to Flers to make gun position Bunter slightly wounded, relieved by Y.29 Batty	
	19TH		Laying Guns 20TH Gr Bunter On Sunken Rd. making positions tenable. Gr Patrie wounded	

249 Wt. W14957/Mg0 750,000 1/16 J.B.C. & A. Forms/C.2118/12.

Army Form C. 2118.

WAR DIARY
or
INTELLIGENCE SUMMARY Z.29.T.M.B. (Cont'd)

(Erase heading not required.)

Place	Date	Hour	Summary of Events and Information	Remarks and references to Appendices
	21st		Returned to S.15.C	
	22nd to 25th		Nothing to report.	
	26th		2nd Lt G.D. East reported sick 27th proceeded to Rest Camp.	
	27th		2nd Lt G.D. East 2nd Lt G.N. East proceeded to forward 2nd Lt Battery M.T. took over Jo. of J Battery. Battery proceeded to position relieving X 29 Battery at 4.30pm. Lieut Wylie joining the battery temporarily.	
	28th		Battery in action fired 40 rounds cutting wire and blowing sap up	
	29th		Same target fired 44 rounds finishing up with 40s 293 guns out of action. A premature from #4 gun killed No. 11200 Bdr Taylor H & attributed casualties to exceedingly bad weather with incessant rain.	
	30th		Relieved by Y.29 Battery Lt Wylie staying with them. Nothing to report.	
	31st		Proceeded to Albert.	

Lionel Walter
Lieut R.L.

29th Division.

"V" 29 HEAVY TRENCH MORTAR BATTERY

NOVEMBR 1 9 1 6

Vol 3

CONFIDENTIAL

WAR DIARY

OF

V/29 Heavy Trench Mortar Battery

From 1st Nov 1916 to 30th Nov 1916

(Volume 4)

Army Form C. 2118.

WAR DIARY
or
INTELLIGENCE SUMMARY
(Erase heading not required.)

Place	Date	Hour	Summary of Events and Information	Remarks and references to Appendices
Quarry Amn. Dump.	1.11.16 to 25.11.16		1 Officer 30 O.R's attached for duty to O.C. Quarry Amn Dump	S.22.
	6.11.16 to 20.11.16		1 Officer, 2 N.C.O's 14 men attached for duty to O.C. 12th Divl. Amn Dump	S.22.
	4.11.16		Fur Coats issued to wounted NCOs. states per attached list.	
	7.11.16		Promotions of NCOs per attached list.	
	16.11.16		Pay issued to Bty.	
E.27.a.10.10	26.11.16		Batty. moved to E.27.a.10.10 - by hand to MEAULTE - marched to Camp.	
	27."		Bty. in huts at E.27.a.10.10.	
DAOURS	28."		Bty. moved hy G.S. Wagon to DAOURS - billets - hutments	
	29-30		Bty. being re-equipped with Clothing etc in DAOURS.	

[Casualties as per attached]

W.H. Gaird 2nd Lt R.F.A.
Cmdg V.29 H.T.M.B.

Casualty Report

To accompany A.F.C. 2118   War Diary   November 1916

Date	Rk, Name	Nature of Casualty	Remarks
5/11/16	Gr. Fagg W.	Attached to 29th Div. Train	
6/11/16	Gr. Dean R.H.	Posted to 2nd Army Travel Workshop	
8/11/16	Cpl. Offer H.	Evacuated Sick	
8/11/16	Cpl. Webb G.	Joined from Base	
9/11/16	Gr. Fagg W.	Rejoined from 29th Div Train	
9/11/16	Br. Ratcliffe T.	Attached to 29th Div Train	
11/11/16	Gr. Cummins E.	Admitted to Hospital, sick	
12/11/16	Gr. Hopkins F.	Evacuated C.C.S.	
12/11/16	Gr. Burn W.	Attached Town Major RIBEMONT	
12/11/16	Gr. Fagg W.	Attached Town Major RIBEMONT	
12/11/16	Br. Ratcliffe T., Grs Jones W. & W. Quelch, F. Cottrell E. Grey M. Morley C. Linney P.	Attached to 29th T.M. Brigade H.Qrs	
19/11/16	Gr. Becker H.	Attached 29th Div Train	
20/11/16	Gr. Hopkins F.	Rejoined from Hospital	
22/11/16	Cpl. McLean A., Gr. Jackson E.	Granted 1 Month's leave to England	
24/11/16	Gr. Jones W. Evans H., Gr. Jackson E., Gr. Miller P. Quinn C.	Reposted to 29th D.A.C.	
	Gr. Watson E. J., " Langston W., " McCrory W.	Reposted to 92nd Bty R.F.A.	
29/11/16	Cpl. Nunn E., Br. Fisher J.	Granted leave to England	
29/11/16	2/Lt. Beeman J.P.	Transferred to X T.M.B.	

To accompany A.F.C. 2118   War Diary   November 1916

29th Division.

"X" 29   TRENCH MORTAR BATTERY

NOVEMBER 1 9 1 6

CONFIDENTIAL

WAR DIARY

OF

X/29 Trench Mortar Battery

From 1st Nov 1916 to 30th Nov 1916.

(Volume No 4)

To
Headquarters
29th Div Arty

**HEADQUARTERS,
29th DIVISIONAL
AMMUNITION COLUMN.**
No. 614
Date 6/12/16.

With reference to this Office No. 601 d/2/12/16 the War Diary of X/29 TMB has just come to hand and is enclosed herewith

Harold Rhodes
Lt.

6/12/16
for LIEUT. COLONEL,
COMDG. 29 DIVISIONAL AMMUNITION-COLUMN.

H.Q. 29th. Div a.

forwarded.

**HEADQUARTERS,
29th DIVISIONAL
ARTILLERY.**
No. S.G. 4297
Date 6/12/16

Day Stukes
Capt
for Comdg. 29th Div arty

Army Form C. 2118.

WAR DIARY
or
INTELLIGENCE SUMMARY.
(Erase heading not required.)

NOVEMBER

Instructions regarding War Diaries and Intelligence Summaries are contained in F. S. Regs., Part II. and the Staff Manual respectively. Title pages will be prepared in manuscript.

Place	Date	Hour	Summary of Events and Information	Remarks and references to Appendices
ALBERT	Nov. 1916 1		Personnel of Battery in billets.	Amd
"	2		Inspection of Battery. Cleaning of guns, belts, stores etc. 1000 ft drawn from F. Cachw.	
"	3		Battery parade from 7.30–9.30 a.m. Battery paid at 11 a.m.	L.N. Lieut
"	4		Cleaning of guns & stores	2nd Lieut Parsons Lt
"	5			2nd Lieut Parsons Lt
"	6		Inspection of Brigade by Genl Peake	A.R. Peake Sintt 2nd Lt
"	7		Signalling Parades at 9.30 a.m. and 2 p.m.	A.R.G.S
"	8		Church Parade	ARPS
"	9		Parades at 9.30 a.m. and 2 p.m. Signalling and cleaning of guns & stores.	ARPS
"	10		"	ARPS
"	11		"	ARGS
"	12		"	ARGS
"	13		"	ARPS
DAOURS	14		Moved to DAOURS in motor lorries. Personnel of battery in billets.	ARPS
"	15		Parades at 9.30 a.m. and 2 p.m.	ARGS
"	16		"	ARPS

WAR DIARY
or
INTELLIGENCE SUMMARY.

(Erase heading not required.)

Army Form C. 2118.

NOVEMBER.

Place	Date	Hour	Summary of Events and Information	Remarks and references to Appendices
DAOURS	Nov. 17.		Started to dig practice positions outside the town.	A.R.G-S.
"	18.		Continued work on the position	A.R.G-S.
"	19.		"	A.R.G-S.
"	20.		"	A.R.G-S.
"	21.		Fired 10 rounds unfuzed to register target.	A.R.G-S.
"	22.		Fired 10 rounds registration	A.R.G-S.
"	23.		Fired 25 live rounds at wire entanglements and a small trench. General Peake watched the firing. Bdr Marland was killed, Lieut. Parsons and Gnr Oliver wounded by a premature.	A.R.G-S.
"	24.		Bdr Marland buried in the military cemetery at DAOURS.	A.R.G-S.
"	25.		Worked on the gun position.	A.R.G-S.
"	26.		Church parade at Divisional School.	A.R.G-S.
"	27.		Continued work on the gun position	A.R.G-S.
"	28.		"	A.R.G-S.
"	29.		"	A.R.G-S.
"	30.		Battery paid at 11.15. a.m.	A.R.G-S.

Instructions regarding War Diaries and Intelligence Summaries are contained in F. S. Regs., Part II. and the Staff Manual respectively. Title pages will be prepared in manuscript.

29th Division.

"Y" 29 TRENCH MORTAR BATTERY

NOVEMBER 1 9 1 6

CONFIDENTIAL

WAR DIARY

OF

Y/29 Trench Mortar Battery

From 1st Nov 1916 to 30th Nov 1916

(Volume No 4)

Vol 4

Army Form C. 2118.

WAR DIARY
or
INTELLIGENCE SUMMARY.
(Erase heading not required.)

Instructions regarding War Diaries and Intelligence Summaries are contained in F.S. Regs., Part II. and the Staff Manual respectively. Title pages will be prepared in manuscript.

Place	Date	Hour	Summary of Events and Information	Remarks and references to Appendices
ALBERT	1	hospital		(sgd)
"	2		In billets Albert. General fatigues.	
"	3		do	
"	4		do	
"	5		do	
"	6		Instruction in signalling commenced. Inspection by CRA 3.30 PM.	
"	7		do	
"	8		do	
"	9		do	
"	10		Church Parade 9.30 AM.	
"	12		do	
"	13		do	
DAOURS	14		Left for DAOURS & from practice Camp.	
"	15		In billets	
"	16		Commenced clipping grim-polo	
"	17			A L Boyle Lt RFA Y21 T.M.B.

T2134. Wt. W708—776. 500000. 4/15. Sir J. C. & S.

Army Form C. 2118.

WAR DIARY
or
INTELLIGENCE SUMMARY.
(Erase heading not required.)

Instructions regarding War Diaries and Intelligence Summaries are contained in F.S. Regs., Part II. and the Staff Manual respectively. Title pages will be prepared in manuscript.

Place	Date	Hour	Summary of Events and Information	Remarks and references to Appendices
SAOURS	November 1915			
	18		Digging gunpits.	
	19		Practice commenced. Drills only fired.	
	20		Preparing Target. Bracket wire R.	
	21		Do Do	
	22		Target finished.	
	23		Demonstration for CRA	
	24		General parade.	
	25		Repairing gunpits.	
	26		Church parade.	
	27		General fatigues & signalling.	
	28		Digging out Dubs on the range.	
	29		Signalling &c.	
	30		First few rounds for Chalford & to instruct new officers in the Brigade	

A. Doyle. Lt. RFA
Y29 T.M.B.

29th Division.

"Z" 29 TRENCH MORTAR BATTERY

NOVEMBER 1 9 1 6

Vol 3

CONFIDENTIAL

WAR DIARY

OF

Z/29 Trench Mortar Battery

From 1st Nov 1916 to 30th Nov 1916

(Volume 4)

Army Form C. 2118.

WAR DIARY
or
INTELLIGENCE SUMMARY   Z.29 T.M. Battery

(Erase heading not required.)

Place	Date	Hour	Summary of Events and Information	Remarks and references to Appendices
In the Field	1-11-16		At Albert on Rest.	
	2		Working of importance to report.	
	3rd	7"		
	5th		Inspection by General Peake.	
	6th		Nothing to report.	
	7"			
	8th		Church Parade.	
	9th		Lieut Hayes A.K. attached to the battery.	
	10th		Nothing to report.	
	11th		Battery being overstrung to one N.C.O. & gunner were transferred to 29th D.A.C.	
	12th		Nothing to report.	
	12th		Left Albert for Hannescamp. Snows.	
	14th		At Hannescamp. Started digging gun pits in the battery.	
	13th			
	15th		Reinforcements of 6 Gunners attached to the battery.	
	16th		At gun pits.	
	17th		Weather very bad.	
	18th			
	19th to		digging gun positions.	
	22nd			
	23rd		Fired 22 Rds observed by General Peake.	
	24th		Brigade Journal of an N.C.O. of X.29 T.M.B.	

Army Form C. 2118.

WAR DIARY
or
INTELLIGENCE SUMMARY, Z.29. T.M.B. (Cont'd)

(Erase heading not required.)

Place	Date	Hour	Summary of Events and Information	Remarks and references to Appendices
IN THE FIELD	25th		Weather very bad.	
	26th		Church Parade.	
	27th		At gun positions.	
	28th			
	29th		Nothing to remark.	
	30th		Issued 4 Rds.	

Lieut W. Salmon P.G.A
O/c Z.29 T.M. Battery.

29th Division.

"V" 29 HEAVY TRENCH MORTAR BATTERY

DECEMBER 1 9 1 6

Vol 4

CONFIDENTIAL

WAR DIARY

OF

V/29 (Heavy) Trench Mortar Battery

From 1st December 1916 to 31st December 1916

(Volume 5)

WAR DIARY
INTELLIGENCE SUMMARY

Army Form C. 2118.

Place	Date	Hour	Summary of Events and Information	Remarks and references to Appendices
DAOURS (France)	15th & 10th /12/16		BATTERY in Rest in Billets in DAOURS. Officers attending course on Telephony from 9.30 to 10.30 am and Gunners 2 pm to 3 pm daily. BATHS arranged.	
"	11th Dec		V/9 H.T.M.B. moved for motor lorry to 15th Bde R.H.A. Wagon line at CARNOY. Attached for work to O.C. Wagon line. (Billets in huts)	
CARNOY	12th-30th Dec R		All unemployed men paraded daily from 8.30 am to 12 noon and 1.30 pm to 4 pm employed on road construction thro' Camp & from the lines to water troughs. (Billets) daily by all ranks. Wheeled vehicles & Officers.	
CARNOY	14th 28th		15th Bde Billequipped out to MORLANCOURT — Bde. attached forward to O.C. 17th Bde R.F.A. Wagon line. 1 Officer 40 O.Rs attached of Warwick Bde R.H.A attached to V/9 H.T.M.B. Jan Return	
CARNOY	15th 22nd 29th		Issue of Pay. Casualties as per attached	

2449 Wt. W14957/M90 750,000 1/16 J.B.C. & A. Forms/C.2118/12.

Casualty Report

V.29.A.T.M.B. To accompany ASC 2118 War Diary Dec.16

Regtl No	Rk	Name	Nature of Casualty	Remarks
4368	Gr	Fagg W	Moved to 4th Div	
285	"	Burr W	D.A.C. 9-12-16	
7647	"	Cummins E	Joined from 7 GA Base Depot 4-12-16	Taken on Strength
87193	"	McDonough J	Admitted to Hosp 9/12/16	Sick
20580	"	Barker A	Attached to 29th Divl Supply Coln 13-12-16	
76475	"	Cummins E	Admitted to Hospl 13-12-16 Sick	
16614	"	Bloor A	Admitted to Hospl 20-12-16 Sick	
49346	"	Spencer J	Admitted to Hospl 27-12-16 Sick	
16614	"	Bloor A	Rejoined from Hospl 29-12-16	

V.29.A.T.M.B. To accompany ASC 2118 War Diary Dec.16

29th Division.

--

"X" 29 TRENCH MORTAR BATTERY

DECEMBER 1 9 1 6

X29 Trench Mortar Bty

7 - 2 - 17

To

Staff Captain R. A.

29th Divnl. Artillery

Herewith War Diary, applied for, of the above unit for the month of December 1916.

W Russell

2/Lt. R. F. A

Commanding X 29 T. M. B.

29 Div
no 6.

Headquarters.
29 Division "a"

Forwarded.

11/2/1917.

C H Clarke
Maj for Brig General
Comdg. 29 Div Artillery

WAR DIARY or INTELLIGENCE SUMMARY

Army Form C. 2118.

Vol 4
X 29 T.M.B.

DECEMBER 1916

Place	Date	Hour	Summary of Events and Information	Remarks and references to Appendices
DAOURS	1st	9.30	Inspection by D.T.M.O. Workers in Gun Pits	1/2/P
"	2nd		do	1/2/P
"	3rd		Church Parade at 29 Div's School of Instruction	1/4/P
"	4,5,6	9.30	Workers in Gun Pits	1/2/P
"	7th		Letters & Wires down from Range to Billets	1/2/P
"	8th		General overhaul of Stores & Stores	1/2/P
"	9th			1/2/P
"	10th		Church Parade at Div's School of Instruction	
"	11th	9.30	Left DAOURS for Pommiers Redoubt Camp arrived at 4 A.M. Rested until 12.30	1/2/P
POMMIERS REDOUBT CAMP	12th		Putting up Huts and making Gun Lines	1/2/P
"	24th		" "	1/2/P
"	25th		Holiday	1/2/P
"	26th	9.30	Left Pommiers Redoubt Camp for T.M. School at VAUX arrived at 4 A.M.	1/2/P
VAUX	27th	9.30	Cleaning Guns & Tour of Gun over lecture for all N.C.O's & Gunners	1/2/P
"	28th	9.30	Gun Pit diggers & Gun Drill. Afternoon lectures for N.C.O's.	1/2/P
"	29th		3 guns Gun Drill firing emptied rounds, 1 Pit each afternoon lectures officers and Recces	1/2/P
"	30th		Firing with Rifleurs, officers put Rounds and Marching Drill	1/2/P
"	31st		Gun Drill carrying Round for Gun pit putting Gun Pit in working order	

29th Division.

"Y" 29   TRENCH MORTAR BATTERY

DECEMBER 1 9 1 6

Vol 5

CONFIDENTIAL

WAR DIARY

of

Y/29 Trench Mortar Battery

From 1st December 1916 to 31st December 1916

(Volume 5)

Army Form C. 2118.

Y/1. 2 French Motor Battery

WAR DIARY
or
INTELLIGENCE SUMMARY
(Erase heading not required.)

Instructions regarding War Diaries and Intelligence Summaries are contained in F. S. Regs., Part II. and the Staff Manual respectively. Title Pages will be prepared in manuscript.

Place	Date	Hour	Summary of Events and Information	Remarks and references to Appendices
Arras	1/12/16		Parade 9.30 AM	
"	2/12/16		" 9.30 AM	
"	3/12/16		Church Parade 10.30 AM. General Police etc.	
"	4/12/16		Parade 9.30 AM	
"	5/12/16		"	
"	6/12/16		"	
"	7/12/16		"	
"	8/12/16		"	
"	9/12/16		" — Cleaning up guns etc & bringing down	
"	10/12/16		"	
"	11/12/16		Sub Sec: Sus Fidi, Popovici, Radovict reported for duty to 14th IDE for duty.	
Bouzi Rosoudnuj	12/12/16		Building huts & dig gun wagon lines for 147 IDE.	
	13/12/16		"	
	14/12/16		"	
	15/12/16		"	
	16/12/16		"	
	17/12/16		"	

Jas Marshall

Army Form C. 2118.

WAR DIARY
or
INTELLIGENCE SUMMARY

(Erase heading not required.)

1/1/29 Tunnel Coy? 1847.

Instructions regarding War Diaries and Intelligence Summaries are contained in F. S. Regs., Part II. and the Staff Manual respectively. Title Pages will be prepared in manuscript.

Place	Date	Hour	Summary of Events and Information	Remarks and references to Appendices
London Booth	18/1/16		Building huts & digging ways in line for 147 & 13 BDE.	
	19/1/16		" "	
	20/1/16		" "	
	21/1/16		" "	
	22/1/16		" "	
	23/1/16		" "	
	24/1/16		" "	
	25/1/16		" " & new qr Hy for Reserve	
	26/1/16		" "	
	27/1/16		" "	
	28/1/16		" "	
	29/1/16		" "	
	30/1/16		" "	
	31/1/16		" "	

Jacobs
2nd Lt.

29th Division.

—

"Z" 29 TRENCH MORTAR BATTERY

DECEMBER 1 9 1 6

Vol 4

CONFIDENTIAL

WAR DIARY

of

Z/29 Trench Mortar Battery

From 1st December 1916 to 31st December 1916

(Volume 5)

Army Form C. 2118.

WAR DIARY or INTELLIGENCE SUMMARY

Z29 T.M. By.

(Erase heading not required.)

Place	Date	Hour	Summary of Events and Information	Remarks and references to Appendices
THE	1/12/16		At Daours on rest.	
	to		Nothing of importance to report.	
	10th		Lieut Haynes A.E. transferred to X29 T.M. Bty.	
	11th		Lieut Walker D.S.H. trans ferred from X29 T.M. Bty to Z29 T.M.B.	
	11th		Nothing to report.	
	12th			
	13th		Lieut Daours for 4th Army Trench Mortars School	
	14th		for ten days course of instructions.	
	14th			
	20th			
	24th		Left 4th Army Trench Mortar School for the 147 Bde.	
	24th		Joined for General fatigue.	
	25th		Attached to the 147 Bde for General fatigue.	
	to			
	31st			

Lieut Walker D.S.H.
OC Z29 T.M. Battery.

2449 Wt. W14957/M90 750,000 1/16 J.B.C. & A. Forms/C.2118/12.

Vol 5

CONFIDENTIAL

WAR DIARY

OF

V/29 Heavy Trench Mortar Battery

From 1st January 1917 to 31st January 1917

(Volume 6)

WAR DIARY
or
INTELLIGENCE SUMMARY

(Erase heading not required.)

Army Form C. 2118.

Place	Date	Hour	Summary of Events and Information	Remarks and references to Appendices
CARNOY (Somme)	Jan 1/17		Fatigue party on Road Construction for 17th Bde Wagon Lines	Appx
"	2.1.17		Battery Employed on Road Construction for 17th Bde RFA Wagon Lines	Appx
"	3.1.17		"	S. Reynolds Gentleman Appx Highland
"	4.1.17		Road Construction fatigue. 1 Bear Winglaw Joining Bty	Appx
"	5.1.17		" M.Cos sent to School of J Mortars	WWC
"	6.1.17		"	WWC
"	7.1.17		Church Parade.	WWC
"	8.1.17		Road Construction fatigue	WWC
"	9.1.17		"	WWC
"	10.1.17		" MWorks sent to Baths at FRICOURT	WWC
"	11.1.17		" Gas helmet inspection. R.1.79.	WWC
"	12.1.17		" 15 men sent for duty to 26th Battery for 8 days	WWC
"	13.1.17		" Bathing Party (weekly)	WWC
"	14.1.17		" 2 O.R's sent to Rest M.O. 29 th R.F.A. to COMBLES	WWC
"	15.1.17		12 men returned from 26th Bde R.F.A. Road fatigues	WWC
"	16.1.17		20 N.C.Os and men sent to R.T.M.O. at COMBLES. Fatigues under R.T.M.O.	WWC

Army Form C. 2118.

WAR DIARY
or
INTELLIGENCE SUMMARY

(Erase heading not required.)

Instructions regarding War Diaries and Intelligence Summaries are contained in F. S. Regs., Part II. and the Staff Manual respectively. Title Pages will be prepared in manuscript.

Place	Date	Hour	Summary of Events and Information	Remarks and references to Appendices
COMBLES	17.1.17		Hdqrs moved to COMBLES.	W.T.C.
	18.1.17		Fatigues to Trenches & Dugout construction	W.T.C.
	19.1.17		Trench & Camp fatigues. 1 Leave to England.	W.T.C.
	20.1.17		Battery moved to TRANOY.	W.T.C.
	21.1.17		1 Officer 39 ORs moved to MONTAUBAN under orders of Staff Capt. 1st Army. Fatigues. Some off party.	W.T.C.
	22.1.17		Trench Fatigues.	W.T.C.
	23.1.17		" "	W.T.C.
	24.1.17		" " 1 hour.	W.T.C.
	25.1.17		" " Party resting heat.	W.T.C.
	26.1.17		" "	W.T.C.
	27.1.17		" " returned to TRANOY Camp.	W.T.C.
	28.1.17		Officer & 39 ORs returned to TRANOY Camp.	W.T.C.
	29.1.17		Some of Bay.	W.T.C.
	30.1.17		Trenches & Camp fatigues.	W.T.C.
	31.1.17		Casualties for month as per attached. W.Heath's Captures. O.C. V.g H.T.43.	

2449 Wt. W14957/M90 750,000 1/16 J.B.C. & A. Forms/C.2118/12.

Casualty Report

V.29 H.T.M.B. & company A.T.C 2/8 War Diary

Regt No	Rk	Name	Nature of casualty	Remarks
49666	Gr	Reynolds A	Granted leave to U.K 3/1/17	
26742	"	Lord J	" " 6/1/17	
38099	Cpl	Mann C	Attached to T.M School for instruction from 5/1/17	
82193	Gr	McDonough J	Rejoined from Hospt 7/1/17	
294	"	Griffiths W.	} Joined from 29th	
251	"	Hopkins R.	} D.A.C. 6/1/17	
336	"	Hutton W.	} Posted to 29 D.A.C.	
61449	"	Swain C	8/1/17	
62668	"	Turner W.	Admitted to Hospt 11/1/17 (sick)	
49349	"	Spencer T.	Rejoined from Hospt 13/1/17	
80319	"	Barry C.	Granted leave 17/1/17	
80089	"	Page J.	— " — 18/1/28/1/17	
81155	"	Bryant P	— " — 19/1/29/1/17	
25484	Bo	Aspinall J	— " — 20/1/30/1/17	
38099	Cpl	Mann C	Rejoined from T.M. Sch. 15/1/17	
95622	Gr	Swain W	Admitted to Hospt 21/1/17 (sick)	
80510	"	Jones B.	Granted leave 23/1/6/2/17	
93304	"	Hodge L.	— " — 26/1/6/5/17	
62668	"	Turner W.	Rejoined from Hospt 26/1/17	

29-1-17

CONFIDENTIAL

WAR DIARY

OF

X/29 Trench Mortar Battery

From 1st January 1917 to 31st January 1917.

(Volume 6)

Army Form C. 2118.

WAR DIARY
or
INTELLIGENCE SUMMARY.
(Erase heading not required.)

X.29. T.M.B

JANUARY 1917

Place	Date	Hour	Summary of Events and Information	Remarks and references to Appendices
VAUX	1.1.17		Course of Instruction at Trench Mortar School, Vaux	M.S.
"	2 "		do	M.S.
"	3 "		do	M.S.
"	4 "		do	M.S.
"	5 "		do Course ended	M.S.
MORLANCOURT	6 "		Left Vaux at 1000, arrived Morlancourt at 1330	M.S.
"	7		Fatigues, (Roads etc) under 15th Brigade R.H.A	M.S.
"	8		do	M.S.
"	9		do	M.S.
"	10		Left Morlancourt at 1000, arrived Combles at 1500. 2nd Lt W.E.GREY joined Batty	M.S.
COMBLES	11		Fatigues for R.E. carrying timber etc for Corps O.P. at Sailly-Saillisel	M.S.
"	12		do	M.S.
"	13		do	M.S.
"	14		do	M.S.
"	15		do	M.S.
"	16		do	M.S.

Army Form C. 2118.

WAR DIARY
or
INTELLIGENCE SUMMARY. (Erase heading not required.)

X 29 T.M.B.

JANUARY 1917

Place	Date	Hour	Summary of Events and Information	Remarks and references to Appendices
COMBLES	17.1.17		Fatigues for R.E. carrying timber etc for Corps O.P. at SAILLY SAILLISEL	W.J.S.
SAILLY-SAILLISEL	18.1.17		Relieved Z 29 T.M.B. digging Trench Mortar Pits	W.J.S.
	19.1.17		Digging Trench Mortar Pits	W.J.S.
"	20.1.17		Relieved by 20 Division T.M's and proceeded to CARNOY, arrived 2000	W.J.S.
CARNOY	21.1.17		Battery Fatigues cleaning guns etc.	W.J.S.
GUILLEMONT	22.1.17		Arrived GUILLEMONT Ammunition Dump to load Decauville Rly Trucks and to work dumps.	W.J.S.
"	23.1.17		Gnr KAIRIS killed by enemy shellfire at 04.30 at Ammunition Dump.	W.J.S.
"	24.1.17		Continued to work Ammunition Dump.	W.J.S.
"	25		do	W.J.S.
"	26		do	W.J.S.
"	27		do	W.J.S.
"	28		do	W.J.S.
POMMIERS REDOUBT	29		Proceeded to Camp at Pommiers Redoubt arriving at 1300	W.J.S.
	30		Building Camp	W.J.S.
	31		do	W.J.S.

CONFIDENTIAL

WAR DIARY

OF

Y/29 Trench Mortar Battery

From 1st January 1917 to 31st January 1917

(Volume 6)

Army Form C. 2118.

WAR DIARY
or
INTELLIGENCE SUMMARY
(Erase heading not required.)

Instructions regarding War Diaries and Intelligence Summaries are contained in F.S. Regs., Part II. and the Staff Manual respectively. Title pages will be prepared in manuscript.

Place	Date	Hour	Summary of Events and Information	Remarks and references to Appendices
	January 1917			
POMMIERS REDOUBT	1		Making wagon lines for 147th F.A. Bde.	
	2		Marched to MORLANCOURT	
MORLANCOURT	3		Fatigues for 460 Battery	
"	4		"	
"	5		"	
"	6		" for 15th R.H.A. Bde.	
"	7		"	
"	8		R.E. Fatigues	
"	9		To MEAULTE for baths	
"	10		To COMBLES to relieve 9olo T.M.B. Relief completed 1500	
COMBLES	11		Shifted camp.	
"	12		Lt Boyle, 2Lt Bowman and 12 O.R. moved into line at SAILLY-SAILLISEL	
SAILLY	13		"	
SAILLISEL	14		Making gunpits	
"	15		Relieved by 2/29 T.M.B.	
COMBLES	16		Making dug-outs in camp.	

A.J.Boyle, LtRFA
OC 2/29 TMB

WAR DIARY
or
INTELLIGENCE SUMMARY.
(Erase heading not required.)

Army Form C. 2118.

Place	Date	Hour	Summary of Events and Information	Remarks and references to Appendices
COMBLES	January 1917 17		R.E. Fatigues - carrying timber to trenches &c.	(W. entries in A.F.A. 7 to appdx)
"	18		"	
"	19		"	
"	20		Relieved by 20th T.M.B. and moved back to Camp at MINDEN POST	
MINDEN POST	21		Cleaned up Camp.	
"	22		1 N.C.O. and 12 men to MONTAUBAN for ammunition fatigues	
"	23		Fatigues	
"	24		Do	
"	25		Do	
"	26		Do	
POMMIERS	27		Moved camp to POMMIERS REDOUBT. 4 Bowmen transferred to 17th F.A.B.de.	
"	28		Building huts &c	
"	29		1 N.C.O. and 12 men returned from MONTAUBAN.	
"	30		Moving huts to new camp at CARNOY	A/Capt L. REN
"	31		Do	O.C. 29 T.M.B.

CONFIDENTIAL

WAR DIARY

OF

Z/29 Trench Mortar Battery

From 1st January 1917 to 31st January 1917

(Volume 6)

WAR DIARY or INTELLIGENCE SUMMARY

Army Form C. 2118.

Z/297.M.A.

Place	Date	Hour	Summary of Events and Information	Remarks and references to Appendices
THE FIELD	1.11.16		Attached to 147th Bde. Gen. General fatigues.	
	2nd		Left 147 Bde and proceeded to Mortauwart.	
	3rd		At Mortauwart, attached to the 11th Bty bombing huts, cleaning billets etc.	
	4th		At Mortauwart	
	5th		Attached to 15th Bde R.H.A. for general fatigues.	
	6th		Lt. Selling admitted to Hospital. Lt. Walker taking over F/C of the battery.	
	7th		Gunner T Brown of T Battery died on leave in England.	
	8th		General fatigues for 15th Bde R.H.A.	
	9th		Left Mortauwart and proceeded to Combles to relieve guards T M Batteries.	
	10th			
	11th		Proceeded to Maw Dugouts.	
	12th		Attached to R.E.'s for general fatigues.	
	13th		2/L Stephenson attached to the battery.	

WAR DIARY
or
INTELLIGENCE SUMMARY

Army Form C. 2118.

Z.29 T.M.B. (Contd.)

Place	Date	Hour	Summary of Events and Information	Remarks and references to Appendices
	15th		Lt Walker & Lt Stephenson & 11 men proceeded to bring in dugging fire party.	
	18th		Private & men returned from gun pits to Louvencourt	
	20th		Relieved by 20th Division T.M.B.S	
			Battery proceeded to Meaulte - Bect	
	21st		Leaving off billets	
	22nd		One Officer & 11 men proceeded to Montauban loading up ammunition	
	25th		Gunner Edwards proceeded on leave for England	
	26th		Lt Walker proceeded to England, 2/Lt Stephenson taking over. 2/Lt Ellis Gurney	
	29th		Officer and men returned from Montauban to Bonnets Redoubt	
	30th		Cleaning up billets.	

W.J. Stephenson 2/Lt
for o/c Z.29 T.M.Bty

CONFIDENTIAL

WAR DIARY

of

V/29 Heavy Trench Mortar Battery

From 1st Feby 1917 To 28th Feby 1917

(Volume 7)

Army Form C. 2118.

V/29
HEAVY TRENCH MORTAR
BATTERY, R.A.

WAR DIARY
INTELLIGENCE SUMMARY.
(Erase heading not required.)

Instructions regarding War Diaries and Intelligence Summaries are contained in F. S. Regs., Part II. and the Staff Manual respectively. Title pages will be prepared in manuscript.

Place	Date	Hour	Summary of Events and Information	Remarks and references to Appendices
CARNOY	1-2-17 to 7-2-17		Fatigues and Boot Hut erection in New permanent T.M. Camp	WD/C
"	8-2-17		3.9H5" Trench Howitzers Ampleth handed over to 3rd Army.	WD/C
"	9-2-17 to 10-2-17		Work continued on New Camp.	WD/C
"	11-2-17		1 Officer and 18 other ranks relieve V/14th HTMB in action in SAILLY-SAILLISEL. 1 Gun Ampleth taken over from V/14th HTMB.	WD/C
"	12-2-17 to 16-2-17		Work on Camp and on Gun pit in SAILLY-SAILLISEL.	WD/C
"	17-2-17		1 Officer and 21 other ranks rejoin Section in Action.	WD/C
SAILLY-SAILLISEL	18-2-17		1 Gun in Action - Work on Emplacements continued - Construction of 2nd Emplacement begun.	WD/C
"	19-2-17 to 24-2-17		Work continued on 2 Emplacements.	WD/C
"	25-2-17		5 rounds successfully fired on FALL TRENCH. Gun registered.	WD/C
"	26-2-17		2 rounds fired. Both short. Old French Charges (date 1915) Construction continued.	WD/C

Continued:

2353 Wt. W2544/1434 700,000 5/15 D. D. & L. A.D.S.S./Forms/C. 2118.

Army Form C. 2118.

V/29 HEAVY TRENCH MORTAR BATTERY, R.A.

WAR DIARY
INTELLIGENCE SUMMARY

(Erase heading not required.)

Instructions regarding War Diaries and Intelligence Summaries are contained in F.S. Regs., Part II. and the Staff Manual respectively. Title pages will be prepared in manuscript.

Place	Date	Hour	Summary of Events and Information	Remarks and references to Appendices
SAILLY-SAILLISEL	27.2.17		2 rounds with Major English Charges M.T. II fired on PALZ TRENCH - Bed displaced owing to severe deflection from zero i.e. 2° 3 rounds short - Bed relaid lodged on 2 sides	WME
"	28.2.17		Target occupied by British Infantry.	WME
			Casualties as per attached.	

W.R.
Capt. TFRA
Comdg. V/29 H.T.M.B.

V/29th H.T.M.B.   FEBRUARY 1917

MONTHLY CASUALTIES TO ACCOMPANY A.F.C 3118

Reg: No.	Rank	Name	Nature	Remarks
294	G̲r̲.	Griffiths W	admitted to Hosp¹ (Sick) 1-2-17	
	2/Lt	Grey W.E. (R.F.A)	Joined from X/TMB 4-2-17	
294	G̲r̲.	Griffiths W	Rejoined from Hosp¹ 8-2-17	
62668	"	Turner W	admitted to Hosp¹ (Sick) 9-2-17	
81155	"	Bryant P	— " — — " — at Base 3-2-17	
	2/Lt	Stephenson N.A (R.F.A)	Joined from Z/29 TMB 15-2-17	
98124	G̲r̲.	Carter F.S	admitted to Hosp¹ (Sick) 15-2-17	
47080	"	Sanderson J.W	Rejoined from 29th DAC	
94608	"	Stallwood H	17-2-17	
	2/Lt	Leal G (RFA)	Transferred to R.F.C 18-2-17	
98124	G̲r̲.	Carter F.S	Rejoined from Hosp¹ 18-2-17	
472	"	Lothian J	admitted to Hosp¹ 23-2-17	
60668	"	Kirkpatrick J	(Dental Treatment)	
251	Dr.	Hopkins D	admitted to Hosp¹ (Sick) 23-2-17	
2280	Bomb̲r̲.	Harper W.G.	Joined from 460th Battery RFA 24-2-17	
178569	G̲r̲.	Turner W		
178224	"	Firth W	Joined from 29th D.A.C	
120848	"	Tooth W	25-2-17	
2371	"	Evans A		
	2/Lt	Grey W.E. (RFA)	Rejoined from IV Army School	
685	G̲r̲.	Burr W	25-2-17	
24542	Sergt	Morris P	admitted to Hosp¹ (Sick) 25-2-17	
118414	G̲r̲.	Bakewell H	— " — — " — 25-2-17	
3363	"	Hopkins J	— " — — " — 24-2-17	
98124	"	Carter F.S.	Wounded in action 28-2-17	To Hosp¹
26742	"	Lord J.R.	admitted to Hosp¹ 28-2-17 (Sick)	

D. Patchett O/Lt RFA
for O.C. V/29th H.T.M.B

WAR DIARY
or
INTELLIGENCE SUMMARY. X 29 T.M.B

February 1917

Army Form C. 2118.

Place	Date	Hour	Summary of Events and Information	Remarks and references to Appendices
POMMIERS	1st-2nd		Fatigue Party Woodcutting Trones Wood	A.R.P-S
REDOUBT	3rd-4th		"	AR.G-S
CAMP	5th/6th		Fatigue Carrying Lumber for R.B Bty to Trenches	AR.G-S
	6th		"	AR.G-S
	7th		Removal to Carnoy Camp	AR.G-S
CARNOY	8th-9th		Fatigues & Foot Parades at Carnoy camp	AR.P-S
	13th		Parades & Gun Parts Inspection by O.C.	AR.P-S
	14th/15th		Parades & Fatigues	AR.G-S
Sailly	15th		Left Party go to Sailly for Gun Pit Digging	AR.G-S
	16th		"	AR.G-S
	19th		"	AR.G-S
	22nd		Remainder of Bty go to Sailly	AR.G-S
	24th		Digging Pits and general construction of Position	AR.G-S
	25th		"	AR.G-S
	26th		Registered Gun lines & fatigues	AR.G-S
	26-27		" Fired 4 Rds.	AR.G-S
	27th		" 2 Rds	AR.G-S
	28th		" 6 Rds	AR.G-S

CONFIDENTIAL

WAR DIARY

OF

Y/29 Trench Mortar Battery

From 1st Feby 1917 to 28th Feby 1917

(Volume No 7)

Army Form C. 2118.

WAR DIARY
or
INTELLIGENCE SUMMARY
(Erase heading not required.)

Place	Date	Hour	Summary of Events and Information	Remarks and references to Appendices
CARNOY	1.2.17		Mr h C.O and 12 O.R. to TRONES WOOD for fatigues.	
	2		Do	
	3		Do	
	4		Lt WYLIE proceded to trenches west of MORVAL to select position for guns	
	5		Do	
MORVAL	6		Checking gun stores &c. Preparing positions for 2 guns	
"	7		Do	
"	8		Getting up stores &c	
"	9		Guns ready to fire in reply to enemy mortars	
CARNOY	10		Battery not allowed to fire. Men both crews returned to CARNOY. Guns in custom handed over to 20th Division. Lt 10721/E and detachments	Allotted to H.H. by H.Q.
	11		Camp fatigues	
	12		Battery proceded to H.D Army School of Mortars at VAUX-EN-AMIENOIS	
VAUX	13		Course of instruction	A.Hoyts AREA.
	14		Do	O.C. 429 T.M.B.
	15		Do	
	16		Do	
	17		Do	

Army Form C. 2118.

WAR DIARY
or
INTELLIGENCE SUMMARY

(Erase heading not required.)

Place	Date	Hour	Summary of Events and Information	Remarks and references to Appendices
VAUX	24.2.17		Battery returned to CARNOY.	
CARNOY	25		Camp fatigues	
"	26		Preparing for action	
"	27		Camp fatigues	
"	28		All B Co. and men to Divisional Baths at BRONFAY	

A.J. Doyle Lt R.F.A.
O.C. 729 T.M.B.

CONFIDENTIAL

WAR DIARY

OF

Z/29 Trench Mortar Battery

From 1st February 1917 to 28th February 1917

(Volume 7)

Army Form C. 2118.

WAR DIARY
or
INTELLIGENCE SUMMARY

J 29 Trench Mortar Battery

(Erase heading not required.)

Place	Date	Hour	Summary of Events and Information	Remarks and references to Appendices
N	1/3/17		Battery at Bayeux Redoubt	Appx
THE	2nd		Fatigues at Trones Wood	Appx
—	6th		Battery removed to Carnoy	Appx
FIELD	8th			
	9/10th		Building huts & cleaning camp	Appx
	15th		Lt Walker D.S.M & 12 men proceeded to Gun pits	Appx
	16th		2/Lt Stewart & remainder of battery proceeded to Gun pits	Appx
	18th		Digging positions	
	19th		Fired 19 Rounds	
	20th		Fired 17 "	
	21st		Fired 42 "	
	22nd		Fired 22 "	
	23rd		Fired 31 "	
	24th		Fired 10 "	
	25th		Fired 53 "	Appx
	26th		Fired 0 "	
	27th			
	28th			

J.D.Walker Lt R.F.A.
o/c J 29 T.M. Battery.

Vol 8

CONFIDENTIAL

WAR DIARY
OF
"V"/29th HEAVY TRENCH MORTAR BATTERY, R.A.

MARCH 1st 1917 TO MARCH 31st 1917.

(VOLUME :- No. 8)

Withers Capt RFA
O.C. V/29 H.T.M.B

WAR DIARY or INTELLIGENCE SUMMARY

OF V/29th H.T.M.B.

Army Form C. 2118.

Place	Date	Hour	Summary of Events and Information	Remarks and references to Appendices
Sailly-Laurette	14th to 4th March		2 Officers, 20 O.R's in action with 1 gun.	WDC
CARNOY	5th March to 15th		In Camp at CARNOY. No 1 gun handed over to Grenade H.T.M.B.	WDC
MORLAN-COURT	16th		Battery in Rest billets in MORLANCOURT. Signalling instruction. 1 Vickers gun pit constructed for instruction purposes.	WDC
	23rd		Bty. Marched to FRANVILLERS	WDC
	24th		Bty. Marched to FLESSELLES.	WDC
	25th		Battery in rest billets in FLESSELLES.	WDC
	26th		Battery marched to St. ACHEUL.	WDC
	27th		Battery marched to Pt. BEURET-sur-CANCHE.	WDC
	28th		Battery marched to GOUVES.	WDC
	29th		At Rest in GOUVES.	WDC
	30th		Marched to ARRAS.	WDC
	31st		Tour in confield. Heavy T.M. positions taken over from 12 D.T.M.B. Casualties as per attached.	WDC Watson Capt 1st TMFA Comdg V/29 HTMB

V 29 H.T.M.B. Casualty Return

To accompany A.T.C.211? War Diary

Date	Regtl N?	Rank	Name	Nature of Casualty
1/3/17	205	Gunr	Watson A	} Admitted to Hospital Sick
"	94427	"	Horobin W.E.	
2/3/17	251	"	Hopkins D.	Rejoined from Hospl
6/3/17	36742	"	Lord J.R.	"
4/3/17	37423	Sgt	Dingley A.	} Posted to 42nd Div T.M.
"	47175	Br	Ratcliff J.	
5/3/17	3363	Gr	Hopkins F.	Rejoined from Hospl
7/3/17	20872	Sgt	Wilde G	Posted to Z 29 M.T.M.B.
16/3/17	118417	Gr	Bakewell H	Rejoined from Hospl
"	2143	"	Robson W	}
"	11382	"	Richens S.G	
"	185565	"	Shore B.	
"	166416	"	Thompson J.W.	} Joined from Base
"	165116	"	Scott L	
"	140908	"	Spencer W	
"	110636	"	Tearle A	
"	8541	"	Smith J.	
"	1146	"	Sheridan C.A	
18/3/17	205	"	Watson A	Rejoined from Hospl
"	118417	"	Bakewell H	
"	37	"	Cottrell A	} Reposted to 29 D.A.C
"	184	"	Capel J.J.	
"	127247	"	Wood C.	
"	94427	"	Horobin W.L.	Reposted to 14 Bde R.F.A
22/3/17	49349	"	Spencer J.	} Posted to 29th D.A.C
"	32435	"	James W	

W H Earle
Capt. R.F.A
O.C. V.29 H.T.M.B.

CONFIDENTIAL

WAR DIARY
OF
"X"/29TH TRENCH. MORTAR BATTERY. R.A

MARCH. 1ST 1914 TO MARCH. 31ST 1914.

(VOLUME :- No 8)

Army Form C. 2118.

WAR DIARY
or
INTELLIGENCE SUMMARY.
(Erase heading not required.)

X 29 T.M.B

March 1917

Place	Date	Hour	Summary of Events and Information	Remarks and references to Appendices
Sailisel	1st 2nd 3rd 4th		In action	Russell Lieut R.F.A
"	4th		Handed over position to Guards Div and proceeded to Carnoy.	
Carnoy	5th & 6th		Cleaning up fatigues	
	7th & 8th		marched to Morlancourt.	
Morlancourt	9th		Fatigue Clearing up camp, also fatigue for Town Major	
	13th		Parade at 9 a.m. Marching and Rifle Drill also daily fatigue for Town Major	
	15th		2 p.m. " "	
	16th		Changed billets and camp.	
	17th		Digging gun pits and fatigue for Town Major	
	18th		" "	
	21st		Shooting for General Carnet	
	22		Marched from Morlancourt to Franvillers	
	23		" Franvillers " Heulles	
	24			
	25		Rest and Parade for Bombing Instruction.	

WAR DIARY
INTELLIGENCE SUMMARY.   × 2 Y I M B

March 1917

Place	Date	Hour	Summary of Events and Information	Remarks and references to Appendices
	26th		Lt Wallis for St Acheul	
	26th		St Acheul for Count lès Lanche	
	26th		Count lès Lanche for Bezures	
Bezures	29th		Lectures on Parade. Preparing for move into Array	
	30th		Instruction in Bombs throwing at 9 am to 11 am. Left for Arras at 6.5 p.m.	
Arras	31st		Taking over Positions and taking up stores and stores	

Army Form C. 2118.

CONFIDENTIAL

WAR DIARY

OF

"Y"/29th TRENCH MORTAR BATTERY R.A.

MARCH 1st 1917 TO MARCH 31st 1917

(VOLUME:- No. 8)

WAR DIARY
or
INTELLIGENCE SUMMARY.
(Erase heading not required.)

Army Form C. 2118.

Place	Date	Hour	Summary of Events and Information	Remarks and references to Appendices
CARNOY	1917 March 1		General fatigues	
"	2		Battery marched to COMBLES to relieve XTMB, but returned. Returned to CARNOY	All relief by XT H L WYLIE
"	3		Fatigues &c	
"	4		Do	
"	5		Do	
"	6		Do	
"	7		Battery marched to MORLANCOURT	
MORLANCOURT	8		Received new draft. Training &c.	
"	9		Drill and physical training.	
"	10		Do	
"	11		Do	
"	12		Do	
"	13		Do	
"	14		Do	
"	15		Do	
"	16		Changed billets to other end of town	A/ Capt H RFD O.C. /X9 TMB. O.C.

WAR DIARY
INTELLIGENCE SUMMARY

Army Form C. 2118.

Place	Date	Hour	Summary of Events and Information	Remarks and references to Appendices
MARLANCOURT	March 17th 1917		Commenced making gun-pits and setting up targets.	
	18		Do	
	19		Do	
	20		Do	
	21		Do	
	22		Firing in the morning. 5 P.M. Received orders to be prepared to move - Guns brought down from the range to	All within by Lt H. W. ELLIS
FRANVILLERS	23		Marched to FRANVILLERS. (Ref. LENS 11)	
FIESSELLES	24		Marched to FIESSELLES	
	25		Rest. Lecture on bombing in P.M.	
ST. ACHEUL	26		Marched to ST. ACHEUL	
Pt. BOURET	27		Marched to PETIT BOURET-SUR-CANCHE	
GOUVES	28		Marched to GOUVES.	
"	29		Instruction in bombing.	
ARRAS	30		" Marched to ARRAS in P.M.	ARRET for O.C.
"	31		Took over gun positions from 12th T.M.B. Carried up guns in P.M.	Out of of for 12th T.M.B. O.C.

CONFIDENTIAL

WAR DIARY

OF

"Z"/29th TRENCH MORTAR BATTERY, R.A.

MARCH. 1st 1917 TO MARCH. 31st 1917.

(VOLUME :- No. 8.)

Army Form C. 2118.

WAR DIARY
or
INTELLIGENCE SUMMARY

9 Z.29 T.M.B.

(Erase heading not required.)

Place	Date	Hour	Summary of Events and Information	Remarks and references to Appendices
IN	1/3/14		Battery in action at Sailly Saillisel.	
	2nd		" "	
	3rd		Handed over positions + 3 guns to Guards Division. Battery proceeded to Barcy.	
T.M.F.	4th		" "	
	4th		At Barcy, cleaning camp etc.	
F.164D	5th		Left Barcy and proceeded to Morlancourt.	
	6th		Battery at Morlancourt doing Town Majors fatigues and marching drill.	
	7th		" "	
	8th		Change billets.	
	15th		Battery started digging gun pits	
	16th		Digging gun pits, digging gun pits	
	16th		Digging gun pits and Town Majors fatigues.	
	17th		Digging gun pits	
	18th		Digging gun pits & phy sical drill.	
	19th		" " " " (Brutie)	
	20th			
	21st		Fired 6 Rounds for General Ashmore	
	22nd			

Army Form C. 2118.

WAR DIARY
or
INTELLIGENCE SUMMARY

D729 T.M.B. (Contd)

(Erase heading not required.)

Place	Date	Hour	Summary of Events and Information	Remarks and references to Appendices
In	23rd		Battery left Morlancourt for Franvillers.	
	24th		Left Franvillers for Fusilliers.	
IWK	25th		Resting at Fusilliers. Lecture on bombs.	
	26th		Left Fusilliers for Saints Acheul.	
LNR.D	27th		Left Saints Acheul for Bouret-Sur-Lauche.	
	28th		Left Bouret-Sur-Lauche for Gouves.	
	29th		At Gouves. Stong Town Majors fatigues.	
	30th		Left Gouves proceeded to Arras. Practice on bomb throwing.	
	31st		At Duras.	

F.Whathen Lieut R.F.A.
O.729 T.M.B&y.

F.Whathen Lieut R.F.A.
O.729 T.M.B&y.

CONFIDENTIAL

WAR DIARY

OF

"V"/29th HEAVY TRENCH MORTAR BATTERY.

FROM 1st APRIL 1917 TO 30th APRIL 1917.

(VOLUME: 9)

BW O.H.Craib Capt RFA
O.C. V/29 H.T.M.B

WAR DIARY
INTELLIGENCE SUMMARY
(Erase heading not required.)

Army Form C. 2118.

Place	Date	Hour	Summary of Events and Information	Remarks and references to Appendices
ARRAS	APRIL 1st	—	Working parties detailed to work on pits and dugouts in heavy mortar position at G29 d 90 20.	[518 N.V.E.]
	2nd		Fatigues as on 1st. 400 rounds of Am'n at position prior to taking over from 12 R.B. T.M.B.	
	3rd		4 guns complete drawn and ammunition of 12 R.B.A. B.T.M.B. at 7 a.m. These immediately taken to pits.	
	4th		3 guns in action by 12 noon.	
	5th		140 rounds fired on trenches between G30d 58, G30b 40 and G30d 90 0, G30d 44. 2 bombs failed to explode.	
	6th		115 rounds fired on enemy trench on the same area. 3 " " "	
	7th		No 4. gun. out of action, Bed near support having given way. 40 rounds fired on same target.	
	8th		50 rounds fired. All rounds were fired with great effect shown by subsequent examination of areas shelled.	
	9th		40 O.R's formed carrying party to take 2" bombs to forward 2" T.M. taken forward by 2/84 T.M.B.	
	10th		Guns removed from pits & parked at Barracks in ARRAS. All complete minus 1 carriage destroyed.	
	11th		Men on Cleaning fatigue. Bore of clean clothing.	
	12th		B.O. Employed on putting captured 5'9" enemy How'r into action at	
	13th-18th		Fatigues as ARRAS.	
	19th		B'y in rest	
	20th		Fatigues on Dump (Ammunition) - ARRAS.	

(All entries by W.J. Hand Capt. R.F.A.
O.C. V/9 T.M.B.)

Army Form C. 2118.

WAR DIARY
INTELLIGENCE SUMMARY
(Erase heading not required.)

Instructions regarding War Diaries and Intelligence Summaries are contained in F. S. Regs., Part II. and the Staff Manual respectively. Title Pages will be prepared in manuscript.

Place	Date	Hour	Summary of Events and Information	Remarks and references to Appendices
AR.R.H.Q.	April 20th	—	Fatigues on Am'n Dump. 20 O.R.'s reported by rota to 17th Bde. R.F.A.; 4 O.R.'s to 15th Bde R.F.A.	
	21st		Fatigues.	
	22nd		10 O.R.'s proceed to 17th Bde R.F.A. for duty.	
	23rd		Nil.	
	24th		Fatigues on Amm'n dump in A.R.R.H.Q.	
	25th		2/Lt Grey temporary attached to 13th Bde R.F.A.	
	26th-30th		Nil.	

Casualties as per attached.

All returns & recommendations made by

Capt W. Thais R.F.A.
O.C. V.29 A.T./4.B.

Casualty Report

V.29 H.T.M.B.   April 1917

To accompany A.F.C 2118 War Diary

No.	Rk	Name	Nature of Casualty	Remarks
3363	Gr	Hopkins F.	To Hospital (Wounded) 4-4-17	
185565	"	Shore R	To Hospt (Sick) 6-4-17	
185565	"	Shore R	Rejoined from Hospl 8-4-17	
49666	Br	Reynolds A	Att 15th Bde R.H.A 12-4-17	
178569	Gr	Turner W.	— " — 19-4-17	
3363	"	Hopkins F.	Rejoined from Hospl 19-4-17	
	20 N.C.Os + men		Att 17th Bde R.F.A 20-4-17	
	4 Gunners		— " — 15 Bde R.H.A 20-4-17	
	10 N.C.Os + men		Att 17 Bde R.F.A 22-4-17	
2143	Gr	Robson W.	Admitted to Hospl (wounded) evacuated 25/4/17	
	Lt	Grey W.E.	Att 17 Bde R.F.A. 26-4-17	
685	Gr	Burr W.		
110636	"	Tearle A.	Admitted to Hospl shell shock 27-4-17	
80089	"	Page F	Admitted to Hospl wounded evacuated 27-4-17	

W.H. Clark Capt. R.H.A
O.C. V.29 H.T.M.B

CONFIDENTIAL

WAR DIARY

OF

X/29TH TRENCH MORTAR BATTERY

FROM:- APRIL 1ST 1917 TO APRIL 30TH 1917

(VOLUME: No 9)

Army Form C. 2118.

WAR DIARY
INTELLIGENCE SUMMARY OF X/29TH T.M.B.
(Erase heading not required.)

Instructions regarding War Diaries and Intelligence Summaries are contained in F.S. Regs., Part II. and the Staff Manual respectively. Title pages will be prepared in manuscript.

Place	Date	Hour	Summary of Events and Information	Remarks and references to Appendices
ARRAS	1-11-17		Digging Gun pits and registered targets	All suffered by Capt H Bereskowf of X/29 TMB. during absence of officer Enjoying attacks to W/Lieut Capt. 17/38th TMB (17/38th TMB I.L.A.)
"	2-11-17		Do do	
"	3-11-17		In action on enemy wire - Fired about 150 rounds	
"	4-11-17		" " " " " "	
"	5-11-17		" " " " " "	
"	6-11-17		" " " " " "	
"	7-11-17		" " " " " "	
"	8-11-17		" " " " " " Came out of action at 4.30 PM.	
"	9-11-17		Fatigues for Z/29 TMB taking Ammunition forward - Bombs wounded	
"	10-11-17		Removed guns from position to Battery Billets - Damaged Guns taken to Ordnance	
"	11-11-17		Parade 9.30 AM Fatigues - Cleaning Guns	
"	12-11-17		" " " " " "	
"	13-11-17		Changed position of Captured Enemy 5.9 Gun	
"	14-11-17		Parade 9.30 AM. Fatigues - 4.30 PM Church Service in Billet.	
"	15-11-17		2 Guns taken to forward position but were not used	
"	16-11-17			

WAR DIARY or INTELLIGENCE SUMMARY.

Army Form C. 2118.

Continuation of X/29TH T M B

Place	Date	Hour	Summary of Events and Information	Remarks and references to Appendices
ATRRAS	17-11-17		Parade 9.30 A.M. - Ammunition Fatigues - 10 P.M. removed Captured 77 M.M. Gun to forward position	
"	18-11-17		Dug new position for Captured 77 M.M. Gun - Which was taken over by Z/29	
"	19-11-17		Parade 9.30 A.M. Ammunition Fatigues - B.O.T. attached to 15th Bde R.H.A. 10 other ranks attached 15th Bde R.H.A. Remainder of Battery on Fatigue	
"	20-11-17		Inspection of Mes & equipment.	
"	21-11-17		Parade 9.30 A.M. Inspection and Battery Fatigues	
"	22-11-17		Parade 9.30 A.M. Lecture on Trench Mortars (2") to new men - Checking Stores	
"	23-11-17		2/Lt MOLHOLLAND R.F.A. posted to Z/29 TMB. - Battery on Ammunition Fatigue. Ammunition Fatigues 1 O.R. wounded	Malice by Lt H Barnbrook O/C TMB 1.C. Beginning attacks 67/68 6 Bde RFA Witheratt O/C TMB 9/12/17
"	24-11-17		" "	
"	25-11-17		" "	
"	26-11-17		2 Lt RUSSELL R.F.A. attached to 14th Bde and 1 O.R. - H.O.T. rejoined from 15th Bde R.F.A	
"	27-11-17		Cleaning Guns Fatigues	
"	28-11-17		Battery Fatigues	
"	29-11-17		On Fatigue for 15th Bde R.H.A. also 29th D.A.C. fetching kits	

Withcratt Capt. RFA
O/C. T.M.O. 29th Div R.A.

CONFIDENTIAL

WAR DIARY

OF

Y/29TH TRENCH MORTAR BATTERY

FROM :- APRIL 1ST 1917 TO APRIL 30TH 1917.

(VOLUME : NO. 9)

Army Form C. 2118.

Y 29
TRENCH HOWITZER BATTERY.
No. ....
Date 30/4/11.

WAR DIARY
— or —
INTELLIGENCE SUMMARY.
(Erase heading not required.)

Instructions regarding War Diaries and Intelligence Summaries are contained in F. S. Regs., Part II. and the Staff Manual respectively. Title pages will be prepared in manuscript.

Place	Date	Hour	Summary of Events and Information	Remarks and references to Appendices
ARRAS.	APRIL			
	1st		Preparing Gun Pits & ammunition recesses	
	2nd	3 P.M.	Completed Gun Pits at 3 P.M. opened fire for registering fired 9 rounds, weather very bad for registering owing to a strong wind & snowing. TARGET G30 D30..80	[51 BMR5]
	3rd		Re registered & fired 130 rounds	
	4th		Battery in action & fired 140 rounds	
	5th		Battery in action & fired 150 rounds, Gas shells were fired by enemy at 12 Midnight which dropped close to the Battery's Billet.	
	6th		Battery in action, fired 150 rounds, Had to cease firing for about 20 minutes during the afternoon owing to the enemy retaliating with gas shells.	
	7th		Battery in action fired 124 rounds	
	8th		Battery in action fired 330 rounds	
	9th		Infantry attacked, Lieut Wylie & a party of 40 men carried Bombs & Component parts up to Z Battery's forward position.	
	10th		Brought the Guns out of action	
	11th		Cleaning & checking gun stores etc	
	12	9-30 AM	Battery parade at 9-30 AM. Fatigues cleaning up around Billet.	

WAR DIARY
or
INTELLIGENCE SUMMARY.

(Erase heading not required.)

Army Form C. 2118.

V 29 TRENCH HOWITZER BATTERY.

Place	Date	Hour	Summary of Events and Information	Remarks and references to Appendices
ARRAS	12th		Lieut Wyllie, A.L. posted to Royal Flying Corps. Lieut Calthorpe D. took over command of Y.29 Trench Mortar Battery	
	13th		Battery parade at 9.30 A.M.	
	14th		Battery parade at 9-30 A.M.	
	15th		Battery parade at 9-30 A.M.	
	16th		Battery parade at 9-30 A.M. at 10 A.M. proceeded to Bomb store & prepared 100 Bombs ready for taking up into action	
	17th		2 N.C.Os & 10 men proceeded to Feuchy Chapel for the purpose of shifting 2 7.7 Field guns & ammunition up into action. 2 G.S. waggon loads of 7.7 ammunition was taken up to the position. The guns were drawn out & got ready to be taken up the following night. Hostile shells on and around the roads very heavy.	
	18th		At 8 P.M. 2 N.C.Os & 6 men proceeded to Feuchy Chapel to finish taking up 7.7 ammunition & guns. 2 G.S. waggon loads of ammunition were taken up to Battery position. No gun limbers arrived to take the guns up into action at 1-30 A.M men were ordered to return to their billets. Hostile shells on	

Army Form C. 2118.

WAR DIARY
or
INTELLIGENCE SUMMARY.
(Erase heading not required.)

Y 29 TRENCH HOWITZER BATTERY.

No. ......
Date ......

Instructions regarding War Diaries and Intelligence Summaries are contained in F.S. Regs., Part II. and the Staff Manual respectively. Title pages will be prepared in manuscript.

Place	Date	Hour	Summary of Events and Information	Remarks and references to Appendices
ARRAS.	18th		& around the roads very heavy.	
	19th		Battery Parade at 10. A.M.	
	20th		Battery Parade at 9.30 A.M. 2 N.C.Os & 8 men attached to 13 Brigade R.H.A. for duty.	
	21st		1 N.C.O & 10 men ammunition fatigues.	
	22		Church Parade	
	23		Battery Parade 9.30 A.M. Fatigues cleaning up Guns & Billets etc.	
	24		1 N.C.O & 4 men at Jersey Brow loading & unloading ammunition etc.	
	25		1 N.C.O & 6 men at Jersey Brow ammunition fatigues – 1 Gr. killed in action	
	26		ammunition fatigues at Jersey brow. Lieut Galettoni attached to 13 Brigade R.H.A.	
	27		Fatigues cleaning up billets etc	
	28		Fatigues cleaning up gun stores etc	
	29		Battery fatigues.	
	30		1 N.C.O & 6 men on fatigue	
	31			Above new reinft by No 9 Trench Howitzer Battery being attached. Sgt Parry & officers

W.J. Garde. Capt.
O/C. T.M. 29 Division Howitzer
6/9/15 Y Trench Howitzer

CONFIDENTIAL

WAR DIARY

OF

"Z"/29TH TRENCH MORTAR BATTERY

FROM :- APRIL 1ST 1917 TO APRIL 30TH 1917.

VOLUME. No. 9

WAR DIARY
or
INTELLIGENCE SUMMARY.

Army Form C. 2118.

8 FDB (?) Brit. Mar. Bde (?)

Place	Date	Hour	Summary of Events and Information	Remarks and references to Appendices
IN THE FIELD	14/4/17		Battery at Bruay, cleaning guns etc.	Appx 1/5
		2.30	Inspection Y29 TMB supply gun R.E.	Appx 1/5
		4.30		
	15/4/17	4.30	Rations in readiness for action.	Appx 1/5
		8.30	Battery followed Inf. Div. with two French Howitzers in action	Appx 1/5
		9.30	Losses but were not inquired.	Appx 1/5
			Cleaning and stocking gun stores.	
	16/4/17			Appx 1/5
		11.30	Parade 9.30am Manning guns etc.	
		13.30	Remaining guns captured from the Enemy. 4 guns attached to 8th Rif.	Appx 1/5
		14.30	Parade 9.30 am. 4 O.R.s on ammunition fatigue. Div in forward H.Qns	Appx 1/5
		15.30	Two guns taken to advanced position but were over 6 regiments	Appx 1/5
		16.30	No. 63263 Bomb. King W. killed in action.	Appx 1/5
	17/4/17		Parade 9.30 am ammunition fatigue.	Appx 1/5
		18.30	General 9.30 am. Four Bomb. King D.	Appx 1/5
			Two Off. & 6 O.R. proceeded to advanced positions	

WAR DIARY
or
INTELLIGENCE SUMMARY.

Army Form C. 2118.

of Z.29 T.M.B. (Cont'd)

Place	Date	Hour	Summary of Events and Information	Remarks and references to Appendices
	18th		C.O.R.S. proceeded to Battery positions with an emergency supply of ammunition. Lieut. Walker wounded in leg and admitted into hospital.	H.Mc 2/15
	19th		Registering.	H.Mc 2/15
	20th		Firing on Registered targets. C.O.R.S. attached to Field Batteries.	H.Mc 2/15
	21st		Firing on Registered targets.	H.Mc 2/15
	22nd		Firing on Registered targets.	H.Mc 2/15
	23rd		Attack commenced 4.45am battery proceeded to Arras.	H.Mc 2/15
			2nd Lieut. Stewart posted to H.Q. Battery.	
	24th		Ammunition Fatigues.	H.Mc 2/15
	25.6th		Lieut. Shuckollan A.E. took over command of the battery.	H.Mc 2/15
	27th		Cleaning guns & checking Stores.	H.Mc 2/15
	28th		Cleaning guns & checking Stores. 1 Gunner posted to "B" Battery.	H.Mc 2/15
	29th		Fatigues under 29th D.A.C. Pitching Camp.	H.Mc 2/15
	30th			H.Mc 2/15

HShuckollan
2nd Lieut. R.F.A.
o/c Z.29 T.M. Battery.

Confidential

War Diary

of

V/29th Heavy Trench Mortar Battery R.A.

From: May 1st 1917 To May 31st 1917.

(Volume: No 10).

Army Form C. 2118.

WAR DIARY
or
INTELLIGENCE SUMMARY.
(Erase heading not required.)

Of V/29 Heavy Trench Mortar Battery.

Place	Date	Hour	Summary of Events and Information	Remarks and references to Appendices
ATTRAS	1-V-17 to 31-V-17		Personnel attached to 15th Bde RFA – 17th Bde RFA & 29th DAC	H.S.R.

J.P.Booth
Capt. MC. RFA
D.T.M.O. 29th Div. Arty.

Confidential

War Diary

of

X/29th Trench Mortar Battery R.A.

From May 1st 1917 To May 31st 1917.

(Volume: No. 10.)

WAR DIARY
INTELLIGENCE SUMMARY.

of X/29 Trench Mortar Battery.

Army Form C. 2118.

Place	Date	Hour	Summary of Events and Information	Remarks and references to Appendices
ATHS	1.V.17 TO 29.V.17		Personnel attached to 16th Bde RHA - 147th Bde RFA - 29th DAC.	JFB.
"	30.V.17		Battery re-formed - Fatigues #during Camp.	
"	31.V.17		Fatigues around Camp.	

JFBack
Capt. MA TFRA
IITMO. 29th Div Arty.

Confidential

War Diary

of

Y/29. Trench Mortar Battery. R.A

From: May 1st 1917 To. May. 31st 1917.

(Volume : N° 10.)

WAR DIARY
INTELLIGENCE SUMMARY
of V/29 Trench Mortar Battery

(Erase heading not required.)

Army Form C. 2118.

Place	Date	Hour	Summary of Events and Information	Remarks and references to Appendices
ARRAS.	1-5-17 to 31-5-17		Personnel attached to 15th Bde RHA - 17th Bde RFA & 29th DAC.	J.P.

J.P. Scott
Capt. MC. RFA
DTMO. 29th Div. Arty.

CONFIDENTIAL

War Diary

of

Z/29th Trench Mortar Battery T.A.

From : May 1st 1917 To May 31st 1917.

(Volume :- No 10).

WAR DIARY of X 29 Trench Mortar Bty

Army Form C. 2118.

INTELLIGENCE SUMMARY.

(Erase heading not required.)

Instructions regarding War Diaries and Intelligence Summaries are contained in F. S. Regs., Part II. and the Staff Manual respectively. Title pages will be prepared in manuscript.

Place	Date	Hour	Summary of Events and Information	Remarks and references to Appendices
In the Field	May/17 1st		{2 Offrs & 16 O.Rs attached to 15th Brigade R.H.A. 2 O.Rs attached 17 Brigade R.F.A. 5 O.Rs " " D.A.C 29 Division	MS
	15		Battery re formed.	MS
	16.		making a camp at Achicourt	MS
	17	9.30 A.M	Parade fatigue around camp	MS
	18	9.30	" " " "	MS
	19	9.30	" Battery moved to Race Course ARRAS.	MS
	20		Battery moved 10-2" & 3-9·45 guns to VI Corps gun park Arras 2 O.Rs remaining with guns.	MS
	21		Fatigue around camp	MS
	22		" " "	MS
	23		" " "	MS
	24		Battery moved remaining 2-2" & 1-9·45 guns to Arras.	
	25		3 O.Rs took over 2 guns in line from 12th Division	
	26.		" " "	
	27		8 O.Rs proceeding to Orange Hill for the purpose of making advanced dump	
	28		making Dugouts at Orange Hill " " "	
	29		" " "	
	30		" " "	
	31		" " "	MS

W Whyley Lt RFA
OC X 29 TM Bty
3/5

6/6 W Whyley Lt
OC X 29 TM By

Vol XI

Confidential

War Diary

of

"V"/29th Heavy Trench Mortar Battery R.F.A.

From: June 1st 1917   To   June 30th 1917.

(Volume No: 11)

WAR DIARY
or
INTELLIGENCE SUMMARY.
(Erase heading not required.)

Army Form C. 2118.

Place	Date	Hour	Summary of Events and Information	Remarks and references to Appendices
ARRAS.	5-VI-17		V/29 HTMB. reformed after temporary division of personnel among Field Batteries of 29th DA. from 3rd May 1917 to 5th June 1917.	
	6-VI-17 to 17-VI-17		1 Section forward helping in Construction of Medium Mortar Emplacements in trenches E of ~~Monchy~~ MONCHY-LE-PREUX. (5 days reliefs)	
	18-VI-17 & 21-VI-17		Fatigues at Ammunition Dumps in ARRAS. All Guns handed over to VI Corps.	
	22-VI-17		All 29th TMB Batteries moved to MONTENESCOURT.	
MONTENES-COURT	23-VI-17 to 30-VI-17		Battery in training at MONTENESCOURT. Complete re-equipment of personnel - Rifle Drill - Telephone Class - Physical exercises	

Written by
M Witcomb
W. Witcomb Capt. RFA
OC. V/29 HTMB.

Confidential

War Diary

of

X/29th Trench Mortar Battery R.F.A.

From: June 1st 1917 To June 30th 1917.

(Volume No: 11)

Army Form C. 2118.

WAR DIARY
INTELLIGENCE SUMMARY.
(Erase heading not required.)

Instructions regarding War Diaries and Intelligence Summaries are contained in F.S. Regs., Part II. and the Staff Manual respectively. Title pages will be prepared in manuscript.

X.29 TRENCH MORTAR BATTERY.
No. ....
Date B/4/6/17

Place	Date	Hour	Summary of Events and Information	Remarks and references to Appendices
Monchy	June 1	11 am	Proceeded to Brown line & Relieved Z Battery T.M.B. and carried up timber for gun positions	R'eid to
"	2	9 am	Digging Gun Positions	R'eid to
"	3	9 am	"	R'eid to
"	4	9 am	"	R'eid to
"	5	9 am	"	R'eid to
"	6	9 am	"	R'eid to
Arras	7	2 pm	Returned to camp at Arras Relieved by Z. Battery T.M.B.	R'eid to
"	8	9 am	General Fatigue. Cleaning up camp and stores	R'eid to
"	9	9 am	"	R'eid to
"	10	9 am	"	R'eid to
"	11	9 am	"	R'eid to
Monchy	12	11 am	Returned to Brown line and Relieved Z. Battery T.M.B.	R'eid to
"	13	9 am	Repairing Gun Positions	R'eid to
"	14	9 am / 5 pm	"	R'eid to
"	15	9 am / 5 pm	"	R'eid to
"	16	9 am / 5 pm	"	R'eid to
"	17	9 am / 5 pm	"	R'eid to

T2134. Wt. W708—776. 500000. 4/15. Sir J. C. & S.

WAR DIARY
INTELLIGENCE SUMMARY.
(Erase heading not required.)

Army Form C. 2118.

X/29 TRENCH MORTAR BATTERY.
No. .... Date 30/6/17

Instructions regarding War Diaries and Intelligence Summaries are contained in F.S. Regs., Part II. and the Staff Manual respectively. Title pages will be prepared in manuscript.

Place	Date	Hour	Summary of Events and Information	Remarks and references to Appendices
Monchy Arras	18	12 noon	Handed over Guns Stores and Position to 12th Divn T.M.B. and Returned to Camp at Arras	M'Neill W R Reid lt
"	19	9.0 am	Fatigues in Camp	R Reid lt
"	20	9.0 am 9.0 am 5.7 pm	Fatigues In Camp and Checking Stores and making up deficiencies from 12th Divn	R Reid lt
"	21		Packing up Stores for moving	R Reid lt
"	22	10 am	Moved to Montonescourt	R Reid lt
Montonescourt	23	9.4 am	Parade and Inspection and Fatigues in Billets	R Reid lt
"	24		Church Parade	A Reid lt
"	25	11.0 am 7.0 pm	Physical Drill Gun Drill and Clothing Inspection	R Reid lt
"	26	11.0 am 9.0 pm 7.0 pm	Physical Drill Gun Drill and Marching Drill	R Reid lt
"	27	11.0 am 4.0 pm 7.0 pm	Physical Drill Rifle Drill and Gun Drill	R Reid lt
"	28	11.0 am 4.0 pm 7.0 pm	Physical Drill Gas Helmet Drill and Revolver Practice	R Reid lt
"	29	11.0 am 4.0 pm 7.0 pm	Physical Drill Marching Drill and Rifle Drill	R Reid lt
"	30	11.0 am	Physical Drill Fatigues in Billet and Our Sports and Packing Stores	R Reid lt

Confidential

War Diary

of

Y/29th Trench Mortar Battery R.F.A.

From: June 1st 1917   To   June 30th 1917.

(Volume No: 11)

WAR DIARY
—or—
INTELLIGENCE SUMMARY.
(Erase heading not required.)

Army Form C. 2118.

Y 29 TRENCH HOWITZER BATTERY.
No. ....
Date. 20. V. 17.

Place	Date	Hour	Summary of Events and Information	Remarks and references to Appendices
Contescaux	June 1st till 22nd	—	Personnel of Y/29 Trench Mortar Battery attached to 15th & 19th Brigades for duty	a.g.
	23rd	3 PM	NCO's & Men ordered to report to Trench Mortar Headquarters for reformation of Battery	a.g.
	24th	11 AM	Divisional Artillery Church Parade	a.g.
	25th	9AM-11AM	Physical Drill, lecture on Gun & Gun stores etc	a.g.
	26th	" "	Physical Drill, Marching Drill	a.g.
	27th	" "	Physical Drill, Gen. Helmet Inspection & Drill, & Rifle Drill	a.g.
	28	" "	Physical Drill & Marching Drill	a.g.
	29	" "	Physical Drill, Marching Drill & NCO's Map Reading	a.g.
	30	" "	Physical Drill, General Saturday cleaning up Billets etc & Divisional Sports	a.g.

A Eikew ? Lieut R.F.A.
Comdg Y/29 T.M.B.

Confidential

War Diary

of

Z/29th Trench Mortar Battery R.F.A.

From: June 1st 1917 To June 30th 1917.

(Volume No 11.)

WAR DIARY of 2/29 Medium Trench Mortar By

INTELLIGENCE SUMMARY

(Erase heading not required.)

Army Form C. 2118.

Instructions regarding War Diaries and Intelligence Summaries are contained in F.S. Regs., Part II. and the Staff Manual respectively. Title pages will be prepared in manuscript.

Place	Date	Hour	Summary of Events and Information	Remarks and references to Appendices
Monchy.	June 1st		Digging positions	
"	2nd		Relieved by X Bty & moved to Arras race course	
Arras.	3		Fatigues around camp.	
"	4		Moved camp to citadel Arras	
"	5		Fatigue around camp	
"	6		" " "	
"	7		" " "	
"	8		Proceeded to Monchy & relieved X Battery. Digging positions	
Monchy.	9		Digging positions	
"	10		" "	
"	11		" "	
"	12		Relieved by X Battery & proceeded to Arras	
Arras.	13		Fatigues around camp.	
"	14		50 O.R. Fatigue R.E. Dump	
"	15		Fatigues around camp	
"	9		" " "	

WAR DIARY of 1.29 Jn B. (cont'd)

INTELLIGENCE SUMMARY.

Army Form C. 2118.

Place	Date	Hour	Summary of Events and Information	Remarks and references to Appendices
Arras	JUNE 17		Fatigues around camp.	etc
"	18		Fatigues Jersey Cave.	etc
"	19		Fatigues around camp.	etc
"	20		"	etc
"	21		" Packing stores etc	etc
Montenescourt	22		Battery left Arras & arrived at Montenescourt.	etc
"	23		Parade 9.8 Fatigues around camp.	etc
"	24		Physical Church Parade	etc
"	25		Physical + marching drills	etc
"	26		Physical drill lecture on guns + plates	etc
"	27		Physical + Rifle drills kit inspection	etc
"	28		Physical + marching drills map reading	etc
"	29		-do- Revolver Practice	etc
"	30		Physical drill Inspection + Divisional Sports.	etc

[signature] 2/Lt R.F.A.

[signature] 2/Lt R.F.A.

Confidential

War Diary

of

V/29th Heavy Trench Mortar Battery R.F.A.

From:- July 1st 1917 To:- July 31st 1917.

(Volume No. 12.)

WAR DIARY or INTELLIGENCE SUMMARY

Army Form C. 2118.

V/29 HTMB

(Erase heading not required.)

Place	Date	Hour	Summary of Events and Information	Remarks and references to Appendices
HERZEELE	1/7/17		Battery moved in Motor Lorries from Montescourt to HERZEELE.	L.o.c.
	2/7/17		Billeted in HERZEELE.	L.o.c.
	3/7/17		Moved in Motor Lorries to A12 b Central [Sh 28 B1W] Bivouacd in field.	L.o.c.
Abeele	4/7/17		Camp completed. Shelter trenches dug. 29th TM's attached to Guards Div.n for duty.	L.o.c.
BOESINGHE	5/7/17		Right X moved into BOESINGHE WOOD for Emplacement Construction.	L.o.c.
"	6-10/7/17		Right and Left X's relieved every 3rd day. Progress on 2 Emplacements at B12 a 17/14	W.o.c.
"			and B12 a 20.05 slow on account of difficulty of getting materials to trucks via light Railway.	W.o.c.
"	5/12		Working party details to assist RE's (75th Field Coy) to construct Trench Tramway cement under	L.o.c.
"			Railway Culvert at B12 a 35.40.	
"	13/7		1 Gun in position at B12 a 20.05.	L.o.c.
"	16/7		2nd gun in position at B12 a 17/14.	L.o.c.
"	17/7		19 rounds fired with great effect at CANAL DRIVE + CANAL AVE.	L.o.c.
"	18/7		45 rounds fired " " " at "	L.o.c.
"	19/7		41 rounds fired " " " at CANON LANE at point B6d 65.05	L.o.c.
"	20/7		16 rounds " " " at CANAL DRIVE Junk CANAL AV.	L.o.c.
"	21st		No rounds fired.	L.o.c.

WAR DIARY
or
INTELLIGENCE SUMMARY.
(Erase heading not required.)

Army Form C. 2118.

Place	Date	Hour	Summary of Events and Information	Remarks and references to Appendices
BOESINGHE	22nd.7.17		25 Rds fired with effect at CANAL DRIVE Jn. with CANAL AVVE.	WDR.
	23rd		21 " " " " " " " and CANAL AVVE.	WDR.
	24th		No rounds fired	WDR.
	25th		" " "	WDR.
	26th		25 rounds fired with effect at CANAL DRIVE.	WDR.
	27th		Battery with drawn from the line. Guns to be withdrawn when roadway in repair	WDR.
	28th		At rest.	WDR.
	29th		32 O.R.s 1 Officer constructed portion of road for horse drawn vehicles from	WDR.
	30th		At rest.	WDR.
	31st		25 O.R.s 1 Officer continued road from B12A 2060 to CAPPELBANK at BRA 7010	WDR.
	N.B.		All arms. Carried to position by infantry parties arranged by Guards D.A. BOESINGHE WOOD subjected to intermittent heavy shelling by all calibres of heavy artillery this'out periods of duty in line. Barrages frequently, especially at night. Casualties as per attached.	

All entries by Watson's Capt.
O.C. Vy H.T.M.B.

Casualty List to Accompany
A.F.C. 2118 for Month of July 1917

V.29 H.T.M.B.

Regt No	Rk	Name	Nature of Casualty
10845	Gr	Stead JH	Killed in Action 4-7-17
40345	"	Conway P	} Admitted to Hospl
675877	"	Evans A	} Sick 12-7-17
	2/L	Snowball W	Admitted to Hospl wounded 13-7-17
675877	Gr	Evans A	} Rejoined from Hospl
40345	"	Conway P	} 16-7-16
82193	"	McDonough J	Admitted to Hospl wounded 24-7-17
25484	Cpl	Aspinall J	Admitted to Hospl wounded 26-7-17
111546	Gr	Gray M	To Hospl Sick 29-7-17

W.H.Crail Captn R.F.A
O.C. V.29 H.T.M.B.

Confidential

War Diary

of

X/29 Trench Mortar Battery R.F.A.

From: July 1st 1917 To: July 31st 1917.

(Volume No 12)

WAR DIARY

INTELLIGENCE SUMMARY X/29 T.M.B.

Army Form C. 2118.

(Erase heading not required.)

Place	Date	Hour	Summary of Events and Information	Remarks and references to Appendices
Molinancourt	1 July		Left Molinancourt	Plenty
Hazelle	2	6.30 AM	9.30 AM Parade. Clothing inspection & gas hood inspection	Plenty
Cantraik (Belgium)	3		Moved to Ondank, arrivin about 12 PM. Drew blankets & sitting up.	Plenty
	4		General Fatigues in camp	Recpt
	5		General Fatigues & gas guard	Plenty
	6		Fatigues up the line & camp fatigues	Plenty
	7		by Y By	
	8		Two men & copl. rations for Y By & general fatigues & gun guard	Recpt
	9		4 men on RF Fatigues & general fatigues to remainder	Plenty
	10		2 men & 1 NCO RF Fatigue 2 men few yards	Plenty
	11		ditto	Plenty
			ditto	Plenty
Canal Bank	12		Left camp for line and took over 6,7,8,9 & M Gun pits & 8 x 1 gun Fired	Plenty
			2 rounds from No 9 & 5 fan Vole retaliation	Recpt
	13		Fatigue party carrying up guns & Nos to 6,7 & 4. Observe Savey killed while sitting up pits. Orders issued by for SOS Fired 25 M.B.	

T2134. Wt. W708-776. 500000. 4/15. Sir J. C. & S.

WAR DIARY
INTELLIGENCE SUMMARY

Army Form C. 2118.
07 X/29 T.M.B.

Place	Date	Hour	Summary of Events and Information	Remarks and references to Appendices
Canal Bank	13		From 8 & 9. Enemy raided Canal Bank under heavy bombardment. Raid repulsed. No casualties in Battery.	Rpt 13
"	14		Registered No 4 Gun on wire in front of Canal & Babel Trench. Fired about 25 Rds. Registered No 6 on Canal Tr. 6 rounds. Wood Lt. Co. Nash about S.C. P1 from Enemy & mounted m.t. line. Enemy opened his own line but did not reply.	Rpt 14
"	15		Fired about 30 Rounds from No 4 at enemy wire in Rebel Tr. Registered No 7 gun in Rebel Trench & Fired from No 6. Wood 60 rounds. 2nd Lieut Cecil slightly wounded.	Rpt 15
"	16		Fired about 60 rds from No 4 on wire & strong point in Rebel Tr. Also about 60 rds from 6 & 7 on wire & strong pt. in Capel Trench. Fired about 48 rds from No 4 as strong point & SOS.	Rpt 16
"	17		Fired 20 Rds from No 4 as Strong Point & 33 rds in Rebel Tr Wire. Registered wire in Canal Avenue with No 4. Nadir General fatigues carrying up bombs from dumps.	Rpt 17
"	18		Registered No 7 on wire near Rosseigh Bridge. No trouble. Returned to	Rpt 18

T 2134. Wt. W708—776. 500000. 4/15. Sir J. C. & S.

WAR DIARY of X/29 T.M.B.
INTELLIGENCE SUMMARY

Army Form C. 2118.

Place	Date	Hour	Summary of Events and Information	Remarks and references to Appendices
Anlaik	19		to camp relieved by 56th T.M.	Pheaff
	20		Rested in camp	Pheaff
	21		4 men carrying ration for Y Bty. 3 men & 1 NCO Gas guard. Remainder dug Pheaff	
			a now. Taking up wire for Y Bty. Hard camp about a mile out, to	Pheaff
			lot lk shell fire.	Pheaff
	22		Completed laying of broaches for Y Bty. Threw camp.	Pheaff
	23		4 men carrying rations for Y Bty. 3 men & 1 NCO Gas guard.	Pheaff
Camel Bunk	24		Returned to line. Relieving 56th T.M. Checked ammunition & stores	Wet
			reported dug out dusty.	Wet
	25		Cleaned up guns ? dugouts. No fire carry to kiew hostile barrage.	Wet
	26		1:50 AM fired 2 bursts on enemy front line 16 rds. 5:30 AM	
			General fatigue carryig ammunition from dump. 4:30 AM put	
			in new bed on No 7 reported flew wire on Rabil Tr. 23 rds	Pheaff
	27		Collected all spare gun stores & equipment in No 7 Semi-circle.	
			Took out No 6 bed & put in new No 6. Fired 12 rounds on Canal	
			Support. 1 man detailed on orderly. 5:30 PM enemy reported	

Army Form C. 2118.

WAR DIARY
or
INTELLIGENCE SUMMARY.

of X/29 TMB

(Erase heading not required.)

Place	Date	Hour	Summary of Events and Information	Remarks and references to Appendices
Auid Bask			On being evacuated front line X Battery went over after Infantry patrols, shot one German officer, captured him & other officer & 2 L/Cpl. Cpl. Randall & Gr Bradley recommended. Infantry having gone forward & bullets held the Base all night.	Rcalfs
"	28		Collected guns stores & tools fallen from in No 8 & 9 bomb stores. Detailed 2 men to report to DA as reserves.	Rcuif
"	29		Awaited further orders.	Rcuif
Orchirch	30		Left line about 5.30AM retrieving camp about 7.30	Rcheaf
	31		Parade 9.3AM Inspection DG 2.0 PM a fatigues	Rcheaf

R. Reid Lieut. TMB
Cmdg X/29 TMB

Confidential

— War Diary —

of

Y/29 Trench Mortar Battery R.F.A.

From:- July 1st 1917 To:- July 31st 1917.

(Volume No 12).

Army Form C. 2118.

Y. 29
TRENCH MORTAR BATTERY.
No ....
Date ....

WAR DIARY or INTELLIGENCE SUMMARY.
(Erase heading not required.)

July 1916

(1)

Instructions regarding War Diaries and Intelligence Summaries are contained in F. S. Regs., Part II. and the Staff Manual respectively. Title pages will be prepared in manuscript.

Place	Date	Hour	Summary of Events and Information	Remarks and references to Appendices
Montauban	July/1	6 A M	Left Montauban by Motor Lorries, arrived Meyzich 6.P.M.	J.a.
Meyzich	2	9.30	Brigade Parade. Clothing Inspection, Inspection of Guns & Cleaning Gun Stores	J.a.S.
"	3		Left Meyzich by Motor Lorries arrived Oudeauk	J.h.S.
Oudeauk	4		Camp fatigues & General Cleaning up	J.a.S.
"	5		Battery left Camp for Trenches in front of Boeshinge village. 1 Officer & 1	J.a.S.
"	6		Sergeant mortally wounded	J.a.S.
"	7		Battery in line preparing Medium Trench Mortar Gun Positions	J.a.S.
"	8		" " " " " " " "	J.a.S.
"	9		" " " " " " " " Relieved by Z Battery	J.a.S.
"	10		Returned to Camp 4. P.M	J.a.S.
"	11		Camp fatigues & General Cleaning up	J.a.S.
"	12		Digging Heavy Trench Mortar Gun Position in Railway Embankment in front of Boeshinge village & fatigues	J.a.S.
"	13		Guides & Ration parties for X & Z Medium Batteries in the line. Gas Guard	J.a.S.

2353 Wt. W2544/1454 700,000 5/15 D. D. & L. A.D.S.S./Forms/C. 2118.

WAR DIARY July/17 contd.—
or
INTELLIGENCE SUMMARY.
(Erase heading not required.)

Army Form C. 2118.

Y. 29
TRENCH MORTAR BATTERY.

Place	Date	Hour	Summary of Events and Information	Remarks and references to Appendices
Oudoule	July/17			
	14		Guides & Ration Parties for X & Z Medium Batteries on the line.	J.H.G.
	15		"	J.H.G.
	16		"	J.H.G.
	17		"	J.H.G.
	18	7 AM	Battery left Camp for action in front of Boesinghe village, relieving Z Battery & throughout the day fired 53 rounds on wire and strongholds	J.H.G.
			In the course of the evening 15 rounds were fired on SOS line by No 5 Gun	J.H.G.
			Battery fired 56 rounds on wire in front of Enemy his Trench.	J.H.G.
			During the day No 5. Gun fired the total of 54 rounds on wire.	J.H.G.
			(One casualty. (Gunner Donnelled)	
	19		"X" Gun also fired 30 rounds on Canal Bank	J.H.G.
	20		7 rounds were fired by No 6 Gun on Enemy Dug-out.	
			The number of rounds fired on this day by No 5 Gun totalled #1. the target	J.H.G.
			being same	
	21		Throughout the day No 13 Gun fired 32 rounds on Canal Bank	J.H.G.

WAR DIARY July 1917 contd.—
or
INTELLIGENCE SUMMARY

Army Form C. 2118.

Y. 29 TRENCH MORTAR BATTERY.

Place	Date	Hour	Summary of Events and Information	Remarks and references to Appendices
Andouck	July 17 22		During the day 10.13 Guns fired 66 rounds on wire (front) & were complimented on the good shooting.	J.A.G.
	23		The Battery were relieved by Z Battery at 5 o'clock & arrived at Camp 7.30 P.M.	J.A.G.
	24		General Cleaning up & ration party to carry rations for Z Battery in the line.	J.A.G.
	25		Ration Parties for X & Z Medium Batteries in the line. Gas Guard	
			" " " X & Z " " " " " " " " also 2 men on Brigade Sanitary	J.A.G.
	26		" " " X & Z " " " " " " " " Bomb Carrying Party	J.A.G.
	27		for Medium Batteries in the line consisted of 12 men. We also found Gas Guard. 2 Men to act as guides for Infantry Bomb Carrying Party for the Medium Batteries in the line. Brigade Parades 9.30 & 2.30. Gas Helmet Inspection & Full Church Parade (R.C.)	J.A.G.
	28		A party of 13 men proceeded to Borah ridge Main Road to wreck an Artillery Truck from the main road across the Canal. Brigade Parades 9.30 & 2.30. Two men carried rations to X Battery in the line.	J.A.G.
	29		Brigade Parades 9.30 & 2.30. We also attended Church Parade (R of E) 5.45 P.M.	J.A.G.

WAR DIARY or INTELLIGENCE SUMMARY.

Army Form C. 2118.

V. 23 TRENCH MORTAR BATTERY.

July 1917 contd.

Place	Date	Hour	Summary of Events and Information	Remarks and references to Appendices
Onclean?	July 17 30		Brigade Parades 9:30 & 2:30. We also found Gas Guard.	J.E.S.
	31		13 men again proceeded to Boesinghe Mairn Road to carry out the continuation of the Artillery tracks beyond the Canal Bank. Brigade Parade 9:30 & 2:30. 3 Men to report to Guard's DTMO for fatigues	J.E.S.

J.M.S. Elgat 2/Lieut R.F.A.
Commdg. V29 T.M.B.

Confidential

War Diary

of

Z/29 Trench Mortar Battery R.F.A.

From:- July 1st 1917   To:- July 31st 1917.

(Volume No 12.)

WAR DIARY
or
INTELLIGENCE SUMMARY. of 1/29/80/80.
(Erase heading not required.)

Army Form C. 2118.

Place	Date	Hour	Summary of Events and Information	Remarks and references to Appendices
Merzeel	July 1		Battery left Rendezvous & arrived at Merzeel	
"	2		Camp Fatigues	
Ondank	3		Left Merzeel & arrived Ondank	
"	4		Fatigues at Boesinge	
"	5		" "	
"	6		" "	
"	7		" "	
"	8		" "	
Yser Canal	9		Battery relieved 96th in trenches Yser canal	
"	10		Digging positions	
"	11		" 2/Lt 106 Russell took over temporary command of Battery	
"	12		" 2nd Lt. Clutterbuck & 2nd Lt Russell killed in action	
"	13		"	
"	14		Registering guns 2nd Lt Gale R.F.A. took over temporary command	
"	15		In action "Wire cutting" & destroying strongholds Capt. Allen Wounded	
"	16		" "	
Ondank	17		Relieved by 98th & proceeded to Ondank	
"	18		Camp Fatigues	
"	19		" "	

WAR DIARY
or
INTELLIGENCE SUMMARY.

Army Form C. 2118.

of X 29 T.M.B. (Continued)

Place	Date	Hour	Summary of Events and Information	Remarks and references to Appendices
Ondank	July 20		Fatigues around Camp	M.S.
	21		Moved camp owing to heavy hostile shelling	M.S.
Yser Canal	22		Relieved Y Battery in Trenches	M.S.
"	23		Battery in action	M.S.
"	24		"	M.S.
"	25		" 2 O.R.s wounded	M.S.
"	26		Battery relieved by Y/5	M.S.
Ondank	27		Resting	M.S.
"	28		Making road from Dawney to canal bank	M.S.
"	29		9.30 am Parade to Church Parade etc	M.S.
"	30		9.30 am & 2 pm Parade. canal fatigues	M.S.
"	31		Making road from Boesinghe to canal bank	M.S.

W. Shey Lieut. R.F.A.
o/c of X 29 T.M.B.Y.

CONFIDENTIAL

WAR DIARY

OF

V/29 HEAVY TRENCH MORTAR BATTERY. R.A.

FROM: AUGUST 1ST 1917   TO: AUGUST 31ST 1917.

(VOLUME Nº 13.)

WAR DIARY
OF V/29 H.T.M.B.
INTELLIGENCE SUMMARY
(Erase heading not required.)

Army Form C. 2118.

Place	Date	Hour	Summary of Events and Information	Remarks and references to Appendices
A10 b 92 [Sheet 28 NW Belgium]	1.8.17 to 31st 8.17		Battery in rest at A10 B 9020 and finally at Wafford Camp. ("S'Camps PROVEN") Following fatigues carried out. 1.5.17 12 O.R.'s reported to D.T.M.O. Guards D.H. 3.6.17 2 N.C.O's 14 men on fatigue collecting cheroux telephone cable. 4.8.17 20 O.R's instructing gun positions for B.19. 30 O.R's instructing gun positions for 29th D.19.	W.T.C. W.T.C. W.T.C. W.T.C. W.T.C.
	5.8.17		All guns + stores handed over to Gerard B.' D.T.M.O.	W.T.C.
SINGAPORE CAMP	7.8.17		By moves to Singapore Camp.	W.T.C.
	14.8.17		2 O.R's sent to BOESINGHE + acted as stretcher bearers. 25 K.D.v.s attacking.	W.T.C.
	18/8/17		1 Officer + 20 N.C.O's + men sent to V Army T.M. School for course of instruction. — at VALHEUREUX (Somme)	W.T.C.
STAFFORD CAMP	19th		Moved to STAFFORD CAMP. Battery paid fortnightly. M Sinclair by Captain Laird RFA O.C. V/29 H.T.M.B.	W.T.C.

[Stafford + Singapore Camps, see 'S' Camps PROVEN]

CONFIDENTIAL

War Diary

OF

"X"/29 Trench Mortar Battery. R.A.

FROM: AUGUST 1ST 1917 TO AUGUST 31ST 1917.

(VOLUME. Nº 13.)

WAR DIARY of **X/29 T M B**

Army Form C. 2118.

Place	Date	Hour	Summary of Events and Information	Remarks and references to Appendices
(BELGIUM) ONDANK	1-8-17 to 2-8-17	—	Parades and Camp Fatigues	RC
	3-8-17	—	Removing TM Guns out of line to BLUET FARM	RC
	4-8-17 to 5-8-17	—	Parades and Camp Fatigues	RC
	6-8-17	—	Removing TM Guns from BLUET FARM to TM Gun Park.	RC
	7-8-17	—	Battery Offr ON BNIt and proceeded to SINGAPORE CAMP	RC
	8-8-17 to 14-8-17	—	Parade, physical training, Marching Drill, Camp Fatigues	RC
	15-8-17 to 17-8-17	—	Parades - Instruction on 6" Newton TM. - 1 Officer and 10 others proceeded to BOESINGHE to act as stretcher bearers	RC
	18-8-17	—	1 Officer & 10 other ranks sent to 5th Army School of TM. VLAMERTINGHE. Moved to STAFFORD CAMP - Remainder Parades Camp Fatigues	RC
	19-8-17 to 28-8-17	—	Parades - Camp Fatigues - 1 other ranks & 1 Officer sent to attachment to RE's erecting screens in ABRI WOOD. (PILKEM RIDGE)	RC RC RC RC
	29-8-17 to 31-8-17	—	ditto	RC

Lieut. RHA

CONFIDENTIAL

WAR DIARY

OF

"Y"/29 TRENCH MORTAR BATTERY. R.A.

From: AUGUST 1ST 1917   To: AUGUST 31ST 1917.

(VOLUME No. 13.)

Army Form C. 2118.

Y. 29
TRENCH MORTAR BATTERY.
No. ....
Date August / 19

WAR DIARY
or OF Y/29 TMB
INTELLIGENCE SUMMARY.
(Erase heading not required.)

Instructions regarding War Diaries and Intelligence Summaries are contained in F. S. Regs., Part II. and the Staff Manual respectively. Title pages will be prepared in manuscript.

Place	Date	Hour	Summary of Events and Information	Remarks and references to Appendices
BELGIUM SHEET 19 A.10.b.9.2. Oudank	August 1		3 men to report to Guards DTMO for fatigues	
"	2	8 AM	2 NCO's & 12 men rolling in wire from old field Battery positions Brigade Parades 9.30 & 2 o'clock	
"	3		1 Officer & 9 men making track for Guns & preparing 6 gun emplacements for L Battery R.H.A. 15th Brigade.	
"	4		1 NCO & 3 men rolling in wire from old Field Battery Positions. 2 NCO's & 7 men making Artillery track back of German old second line for 15th Brigade R.H.A. Brigade Parades 9.30 & 2 o'clock.	
"	5		1 NCO & 3 men rolling in wire. 1 NCO & 3 men making Artillery track back of German old second line. Brigade Parades (BE) 12 o'clock. 1 NCO & 3 men for Gas Guard. 1 NCO & 8 men proceeded to Boesinghe to load up Medium & Heavy Trench Mortar Guns & bring to Camp. ~~1 Gunner transferred to this Battery from Y.29 TMBy.~~ 1 Gunner transferred to Y.29 TM Bty from Y Battery. Brigade Parades 9.30 & 2 o'clock. R.C.'s Church Parade	
"	6			

Army Form C. 2118.

WAR DIARY or INTELLIGENCE SUMMARY

(Erase heading not required.)

Y.29 TRENCH MORTAR BATTERY.

M ....
Date August 17.

Instructions regarding War Diaries and Intelligence Summaries are contained in F. S. Regs., Part II. and the Staff Manual respectively. Title pages will be prepared in manuscript.

(11)

Place	Date	Hour	Summary of Events and Information	Remarks and references to Appendices
BELGIUM 28NW A10 G 92 Oudenk	August 7		Brigade Parade 9.30. Guns & Stores taken to Guards T M Brigade Camp Oudenk & 3 men of this Battery left as Guard.	
"Scamps" PROVEN and Singapore Camp	8		Struck Camp at Oudenk & proceeded to Singapore Camp. First Reinforcement Battery at Singapore Camp from Hospital. Brigade Parade 9.30 Camp Fatigues	
"	9		Brigade Parade 9.30 & 2 o'clock. Inspection of equipment.	
"	10		Brigade Parade 9.30 & 2 o'clock. Route March. NCO & 3 men for Gas Guard	
"	11		" 9.30 & 2 " Marching Drill. Signalling Class	
"	12		" 9.30 & 2 " Gas Helmet Drill. Signalling Class	
"	13		" 9.30 & 2 " Instruction in Semaphore & Signalling Class	
"	14		" 9.30 & 2 " Physical Instruction	
"	15		" 9.30 & 2 " Physical Training 11 o'clock to 12 o'clock. One man carrying rations to Guard at Oudenk. Instruction on the 6" Newton Gun.	
"	16	10:30 PM	1 NCO & 9 men left Camp & proceeded to Borehing to act as stretcher Bearers for 2 days. Brigade Parade 9.30 & 2 o'clock. Instruction on 6" Newton Gun.	

Army Form C. 2118.

WAR DIARY
or
INTELLIGENCE SUMMARY.
(Erase heading not required.)

Y. 29
TRENCH MORTAR BATTERY.

No ....
.... August /16 ....

Place	Date	Hour	Summary of Events and Information	Remarks and references to Appendices
"S"Camp PROVEN area	August			
Siegeport Camp	17		Brigade Parade 9.30 & 2 o'clock. Physical Training. Stretcher bearing party returned to Camp. N.C.O. for Guard	
"	18		1 Officer & 9 Men proceeded to 5th Army Trench Mortar School for course of T.M. Moved from Siegeport Camp to Stafford Camp. Battery found 3 men for Guard	
"S"Camp PROVEN area Stafford Camp	19	9.15	Bathing Parade. Church Parade	
"	20		1 Officer & 7 men attached to R.E's for fatigues (forward working party)	
"	21		" " " " " " " "	
"	22		" " " " " " " "	
"	23		" " " " " " " " 1 N.C.O. attached to D.A.C.	
"	24		" " " " " " " "	
"	25		" " " " " " " "	
"	26		Guns & Stores brought from Quarrie Camp Ondank to Stafford Camp. Cleaning up Guns & Stores. One man for Brigade Guard. 36 men attached to R.E's. N.C.O attached to D.A.C. (3 forward working party)	
"	27		6 men attached to R.E's (forward working party)	
"	28		6 " " " R.E's. 1 N.C.O attached to D.A.C. (forward working party) R.E's party returned to Camp	

Army Form C. 2118.

WAR DIARY
or
INTELLIGENCE SUMMARY.
(Erase heading not required.)

Y.29 TRENCH MORTAR BATTERY.

Date August 1917

Place	Date	Hour	Summary of Events and Information	Remarks and references to Appendices
"S" Camp PROVEN area	August 1917			
Stafford Camp	28		2 Men proceeded to Boeschepe attached to R.E.s (forward working party)	20
"	29		Brigade Parades 9.30 & 2 o'clock. 2 men attached to R.E.s 1 N.C.O attached to D.A.C	20
"	30		" " 9.30 & 2 " 2 " " " 1 N.C.O attached to Camp Sahgues DAC	20
"	31		" " 9.30 & 2 " 1 man " " "	20
			1 N.C.O attached D.A.C.	

J. Ritchope, Lieut R.F.A.
Comdg Y 29 T.M. Bty.

CONFIDENTIAL

WAR DIARY

OF

"Z"/29 TRENCH MORTAR BATTERY. R.A.

FROM: AUGUST 1st 1917 TO AUGUST 31st 1917.

(VOLUME No 13.)

WAR DIARY
or
INTELLIGENCE SUMMARY

Army Form C. 2118.

Z/20th T M B

(Erase heading not required.)

Place	Date	Hour	Summary of Events and Information	Remarks and references to Appendices
ONDANK	1st		Parade 9.30am & 3.0pm Genl. Fatigues.	Nil
"	2nd		"	Nil
"	3rd		Removing guns out of the line to Black Farm.	Nil
"	4th		Digging gun positions for R Battery R.H.A. Parade 9.30am & 2.0pm	Nil
"	5th		Removing guns from Black Farm to Gun Park.	Nil
"	6th		Battery Left ONDANK & proceeded to Singapore Camp.	Nil
"	7th		Parade 9.30 am Camp Fatigues.	Nil
Singapore Camp	8th		"	Nil
"	9th		"	Nil
"	11th		Parade 9.30 am & 2.0 pm. Physical Exercise & Marching Drill	Nil
"	14th		Parade 9.30am Instructions on 6" Newton T. Mortars.	Nil
"	15th		Parade 10 O.Rs proceeded to Boesinghe acting as Stretcher bearers.	Nil
"	16th		Parade 9.30am Instructions on 6" Newton T. Mortars. 1 O.R. attached 29 D.A.C.	Nil
"	17th		10 O.Rs returned Battery from Boesinghe. 1 O.R. attached 209 D.A.C.	Nil
"	18th		1 Officer & 10 O.Rs proceeded to 5th Army Trench M School.	Nil
"	18th		Left Singapore Camp & proceeded to Stafford Camp.	Nil
Stafford Camp	19th		1.30am Bathing Parade.	Nil
"	20th		2 O.Rs proceeded to Boesinghe attached to R.E.s (General working party)	Nil

(1)

Army Form C. 2118.

WAR DIARY
of Z/29 T.M.B.
INTELLIGENCE SUMMARY.
(Erase heading not required.)

Place	Date	Hour	Summary of Events and Information	Remarks and references to Appendices
Shifford Camp	20th 10.8.31.7.		One Officer & 10 O.Rs at 5th Army Trench Mortar School. 2/Lt. Gunner Shallicer C. wounded & admitted into Hospital.	W.R. J.S.
			Whey Lieut R.F.A. Z.29 Trench Mortar Battery	

Confidential

War Diary

of

V/29 Heavy Trench Mortar Battery R.A.

From: September 1st 1917 To September 30th 1917

(Volume No 14)

Army Form C. 2118.

WAR DIARY
or
INTELLIGENCE SUMMARY.
(Erase heading not required.)

Instructions regarding War Diaries and Intelligence Summaries are contained in F. S. Regs., Part II. and the Staff Manual respectively. Title pages will be prepared in manuscript.

of 47 N/29 H.T.M.B

Place	Date	Hour	Summary of Events and Information	Remarks and references to Appendices
In the field Belgium	September 1st 2nd 3rd 4th 5th		1 Officer & 26 O.R. undergoing a course of instruction at 5th Army T.M. School (Heavy)	CSW
	1st 2nd 3rd		7 N.C.O.s men attached to London R.E. erecting "camouflage" in A.B.R.1 wood (PILKEM RIDGE)	CSW
	3rd to 20th		2 N.C.Os attached to XIV School BOLLEZEELE to undergo a course of instruction in (Lewis gun) anti aircraft work	CSW
	3rd to 4th		3 Gunners attached to Y & B 75 de R.F.A. to assist in making gun pits (near the river STEENBEEK)	CSW
	13th to 16th		6 Gunners attached to 5th Army T M School to undergo a course of instruction in Heavy Trench Mortars.	CSW
	8th to 17th		1 R.C.L. attached to Gas School at BOLLEZEELE to undergo a course of instructions in gases.	CSW
	16th to 30th		2 N.C.O.s attached to 29th Div Amt Ramp TURQUE-FARM to assist in drawing ammunition	CSW
	18th to 19th		7 N.C.O.s & 4 men attached to A60 B/y R.F.A. to assist with ammunition during a bombardment.	CSW
			During this period N.C.O.s & men not employed as above "Physical Drill" & "Fatigues" daily	CSW

2353 Wt. W2514/1451 700,000 5/15 D. D. & L.   A.D.S.S./Forms/C. 2118.

Army Form C. 2118.

WAR DIARY
INTELLIGENCE SUMMARY.
(Erase heading not required.)

Instructions regarding War Diaries and Intelligence Summaries are contained in F.S. Regs., Part II. and the Staff Manual respectively. Title pages will be prepared in manuscript.

Place	Date	Hour	Summary of Events and Information	Remarks and references to Appendices
Contenoutl:- In the Field Belgium	22nd		Battery moved from STAFFORD Camp to AIRY AGE WOESTON	CRW
	28th		All available W.O's & men employed in making horse standings for 17 PDR Hy CRW	CRW
	29th		1 Officer & 8 O.R. attached to 5th Army T.M. School to undergo a course of instruction in heavy trench mortars	

CWilkinson 2/Lt RFA
for OC V/29 H.T.M.B.

2353 Wt. W2544/1454 700,000 5/15 D. D. & L. A.D.S.S./Forms/C. 2118.

Confidential

War Diary

of

X/29 Trench Mortar Battery R.A.

From: September 1st 1917 To September 30th 1917.

Volume No 14.

Army Form C. 2118.

WAR DIARY
or X/29 T.M.B.
INTELLIGENCE SUMMARY.
(Erase heading not required.)

Place	Date	Hour	Summary of Events and Information	Remarks and references to Appendices
In the Field	1-9-17 to 3-9-17		1 officer 8 other ranks putting up Camouflage at ABRI WOOD. 1 officer 9 OR's attending Course of instruction at V army School of T.M's.	By H
BELGIUM	4-9-17 to 5-9-17			By H
	6-9-17		1 officer 9 other ranks returned from V army School – remainder of Battery on Fatigues on R.E. DUMP ORDNANCE.	By H
	7-9-17		3 OR's Fatigues ORDNANCE DUMP – 5 OR's putting up Camouflage at ABRI WOOD.	By H
	8-9-17 to 13-9-17		remainder of Battery physical exercise & camp Fatigues	By H
	14-9-17		Fatigues ORDNANCE DUMP. 5 OR's digging forward Gun positions for 29th Div arty.	By H
	15-9-17 to 21-9-17		5 OR's Ammunition Fatigues at Gun line for 15th Bde R.H.A.	By H
	22-9-17		Battery moved from STAFFORD CAMP to WAFSTON – erecting Camp.	By H
	23-9-17 to 30-9-17		personnel of Battery erecting Stables and horse standings for 15th Bde RHA 3 OR's proceeded to 5th Army T.M School	By H

Bv. Hubert 2/Lt RFA
for O.C. X/29 T.M.B.

Confidential

War Diary

of

Y/29 Trench Mortar Battery R.A.

From: September 1st 1917 To September 30th 1917.

Volume No 14.

Army Form C. 2118.

Y.29 TRENCH MORTAR BATTERY.
No. _____ Date. _____

WAR DIARY or INTELLIGENCE SUMMARY.
September 1917

(Erase heading not required.)

Instructions regarding War Diaries and Intelligence Summaries are contained in F.S. Regs., Part II. and the Staff Manual respectively. Title pages will be prepared in manuscript.

Place	Date	Hour	Summary of Events and Information	Remarks and references to Appendices
Stafford Camp F6 A15 (Sheet 27)	Sept 1/17 1st		1 Officer & 9 men attached the 3rd Army School of Instruction on the 2" Trench Mortar Gun. The course commenced with Gun Pit digging & Gun Drill. 1 N.C.O. attached to D.A.C. on ammunition Dump. 2 Men attached to R.E.'s erecting Camouflage in front of Gun positions & Aubrey Wood & along Pilkem Ridge.	JABS
	1st		1 Officer was permanently posted to the Warwick Battery R.H.A. 15th Brigade. Brigade Parades 9.30 & 2.0'clock. Camp Fatigues.	ALBB
	2nd		The N.C.O.'s & men attending the school used through the same preliminaries as on the 1st. 4 Detachments fired 20 rounds from the 2" Trench Mortar. Brigade Parade at 9.30. Camp Fatigues. Church Parade (B of E)	ALBB
	3rd		On the morning of the 3rd the men at the school were on Gun Park fatigues cleaning Guns & Gun Stores & in the afternoon Billet cleaning & preparations were made for the return journey. The Party left the school at 6 o'clock P.M. en route for Stafford Camp. 2 N.C.O.'s attended a course on anti-aircraft. Brigade Parade 9.30. 3 men were attached to the 78th Brigade on fatigues	ALBB
	4th		The school Party on the return journey arrived at Abbeville & bivouaced there for the night departing next morning at 10.30 A.M. Camp fatigues	LBB

2353 Wt. W2544/1454 700,000 5/15 D. D. & L. A.D.S.S./Forms/C. 2118.

Army Form C. 2118.

WAR DIARY September 1919
or
INTELLIGENCE SUMMARY.
(Erase heading not required.)

T.&E.I. MORTAR BATTERY.

Place	Date	Hour	Summary of Events and Information	Remarks and references to Appendices
Stafford Camp	Sept 4th		4 + 1 man on duty carrying meal etc. to men in line working on fatigues.	H.B/B
	5th		On this date the travelling party arrived at Stables & spent the night in the Rest Camp. Fatigues etc were carried on at the Trench Mortar Camp.	H.B/B
	6th		The journey commenced for home at 9:30 A.M. & the party after an all day train ride arrived at Poperinghe at 5 o'clock & proceeded to Stafford Camp, arriving at Camp about midnight.	N.B/B.
	7th		1 Man was sent to report to D.A.C. at Ondank Dump & another was sent to the R.E's to relieve one man. At 9:30 a Parade for the whole Brigade was held.	H.B/B.
	8th		Brigade Parade at 9:30. also 1 N.C.O. + 3 men on Guard	H.B/B
	9th		Brigade Parade & general Camp fatigues	H.B/B.
	10th		A party of men proceeded to the firing line & were attached to R.E.'s 55th Coy. Station H. & under their supervision erected camouflage screens in front of Batteries beyond Canal. We also provided a Gas Guard	H.B.B.
	11th		The same work of erecting screens was again carried out & a Gas Guard mounted in the evening.	H.B.B

Army Form C. 2118.

Y. 29.
TRENCH MORTAR BATTERY.

WAR DIARY
September 1917

INTELLIGENCE SUMMARY.
(Erase heading not required.)

Place	Date	Hour	Summary of Events and Information	Remarks and references to Appendices
Stafford Camp	Sept 12		The R.E's party still continued erecting screens & at- dusk a gas guard went on duty	
	13		do	
	14		The remainder of the Battery being on Camp fatigues	
	15		The party still continued erecting screens also finding a gas guard	
	16		do	
	17		do	
	18		do	
	19		The men erecting screens were granted a holiday but a gas guard was mounted in the evening	
	20		A continuation of the above fatigue was carried out & again a gas guard was detailed for duty	
	21		do	
	22		do	

Lieut. S. B. Belcher took over command of Y/Y Battery.

WAR DIARY
or
INTELLIGENCE SUMMARY.

(Erase heading not required.)

Army Form C. 2118.

Y. 29 TRENCH MORTAR BATTERY.

September 1917

Place	Date	Hour	Summary of Events and Information	Remarks and references to Appendices
Stafford Camp	22nd		On the afternoon of this date the Brigade removed to new quarters on the Westen-Oudland Road, near Elverdinghe.	A.1.B.1.B.
A 12 B 6.9 (Sheet 28)	23rd		The R.E. party concluded their work & proceeded back to Head Quarters, arriving at 8:30 AM. They paraded at 9:30 & were divided into small parties & reported to 15th Brigade Head Quarters & were sent to the different Batteries in the Brigade for the purpose of erecting Winter stables. Brigade Parades at 6:15 AM 9:0 AM & 2 o'clock P.M.	A.1.B.1.B.
	24th		The party carried on the work of erecting stables for 'J' Battery R.H.A. commencing at 6:30 A.M.	A.1.B.1.B.
	25th	6:15 AM	The parties proceeded to their respective Batteries & carried on with the Building of the Stables. This Battery also found a Brigade Guard	A.1.B.1.B.
	26th		The same Parades & fatigues were carried out, & the building of sand-bag walls round the Tents to ensure the safety of the men from splinters from projectiles dropped by hostile aircraft.	A.1.B.1.B.
	27th		do.—	A.1.B.1.B.
	28th		do.—	A.1.B.1.B.

Army Form C. 2118.

Y. 29
TRENCH MORTAR
BATTERY.

No. ....
Date ....

Instructions regarding War Diaries and Intelligence Summaries are contained in F. S. Regs., Part II. and the Staff Manual respectively. Title pages will be prepared in manuscript.

WAR DIARY September 1917

INTELLIGENCE SUMMARY.

(Erase heading not required.)

Place	Date	Hour	Summary of Events and Information	Remarks and references to Appendices
	Sept 1/17		3 men proceeded to the 5th Army School for Instruction.	AN212/3
	29th		Still proceeding with the work of erecting stables & building sand-bag walls	AN212/3
	30th		do do	AN212/3
			1 N.C.O. & 3 men formed a Brigade Guard.	

N.B. Belakefield Lieut. R.F.A.
Commdg Y/29 Trench Mortar Bty.

Confidential

War Diary

of

Z/29 Trench Mortar Battery R.A.

From: September 1st 1917 To: September 30th 1917.

Volume No. 14.

WAR DIARY of No. 29 Trench Mortar Battery Army Form C. 2118.
INTELLIGENCE SUMMARY. for Sept. 1917

Place	Date	Hour	Summary of Events and Information	Remarks and references to Appendices
In the field	Sept 1		1 Offr & 10 O.R's at School of Mortars 5th Army	3/4/3/5
Belgium	4		1 Offr & 30 O.R's fatiguing up camouflage for above Wood (PILKEM RIDGE)	3/4/3/5 1/4/3/5
	4		2.O.R's Ammunition dump Elverdinghe	
	5		Remainder of battery digging forward 18" gun positions	3/4/3/5
	6		1 Offr & 10 O.R's returned from T.M. School remainded on fatigue as above 2.O.R's Ordnance dump Stafford camp	3/4/3/5
	7		Fatigue as above, remainder physical exercise, fatigue Stafford camp	3/4/3/5
	15		Do	3/4/3/5
	20		Do	3/4/3/5 A/4/3/5
	21		4 O.R's Ammunition fatigue forward position & by R.H.A	3/4/3/5
	22		Battery removed from Stafford camp to Worsten	3/4/3/5
	23		Building stables for 15 Bde R.H.A	3/4/3/5
	30		Do	
	29		1 Offr and 5 O.R's proceeded to V Army School T.M's for course of instruction	14/9/10

H.O.Bellew Lieut T.M.B
for O.C./29 T.M.B

Confidential

War Diary

of

V/29 Heavy Trench Mortar Battery

From October 1st 1917 To October 31st 1917

Volume No 15

Army Form C. 2118.

WAR DIARY
or
~~INTELLIGENCE SUMMARY.~~

05 1/29. H.T.M.B

(Erase heading not required.)

Place	Date	Hour	Summary of Events and Information	Remarks and references to Appendices
In the Field	1/7/17 to 15/7/17		1 Officer & 9 O.Rs under going a course of instruction in Trench Mortars at 5th Army T.M. School VALHEUREUX	
WOESTEN BELGIUM	17.7.17		Fatigues making horse standings for 171st R.F.A. WOESTEN	
	18.9.17 19.9.17 20.9.17 21.9.17 22.9.17		Assisting 171st R.F.A. at gun positions & with ammunition. Casualties 5" L/c No 3149 Gr. Fogg W + 165116 Gr. Scott L (shell wound)	
	23.9.17		Moving to camp	
	10.10.17 11.10.17 12.10.17 13.10.17		Fatigues in Camp	
			Fatigues making Hrs. standings for 17th Bde R.F.A	
	14.10.17		(7 R.b.a a new fatigues at MAIRIE - JEAN - FARM erecting armstrong huts & fatigues & horse standings	(Woesinghe)
	18.9.17 to 20.9.17 23.10.17		Fatigues on horse standings	
	24.10.17		Fatigues in Camp	
			Entrained at PESELHOEK	
DOULLENS	25.10.17		Detrained at DOULLENS & marched to CAUMESNIL	
CAUMESNIL	26.10.17		Fatigue	

Army Form C. 2118.

WAR DIARY
or
INTELLIGENCE SUMMARY.
(Erase heading not required.)

Place	Date	Hour	Summary of Events and Information	Remarks and references to Appendices
CRUMESNIL	27/7		MM MM Kit Inspection. Fatigues	ww
"	28/7		Church parade & Sports. Baths	ww
"	29/7		Route march	ww
"	30/7		Moved to VAUXL	ww
VAUXL	31/7		Fatigues	ww
			Entries by	
			W.H. Gads Capt	
			& Ng H.T.M.R.	

Vol 15

Confidential

War Diary

of

X/29 Trench Mortar Battery R.A

From October 1st 1917 To October 31st 1917.

Volume No 15.

Army Form C. 2118.

WAR DIARY
or of X/99.TMB
INTELLIGENCE SUMMARY.
(Erase heading not required.)

Instructions regarding War Diaries and Intelligence Summaries are contained in F.S. Regs., Part II. and the Staff Manual respectively. Title pages will be prepared in manuscript.

Place	Date	Hour	Summary of Events and Information	Remarks and references to Appendices
WOESTEN	Oct. 1st		1 Officer and 12 ORs fatigues for 15th H.A. Bde Waggon Line.	Bn H.
	2nd		"	Bn H
	3rd		11 ORs "	Bn H
	4d		" "	Bn H
	5d		9 ORs digging gun positions for 17th F.A. Bde. 2 ORs Ammunition dump fatigues	Bn H
	6d		19 ORs " "	Bn H
	7d		" "	Bn H
	8th		" "	Bn H
	9d		" moving and building camp "	Bn H
	10d		" "	Bn H
	11d		9 & 10 ORs building & repairing stables for 15th H.A. Bde	Bn H
	12d		8 & 11 ORs "	Bn H
	13d		9 & 12 ORs "	Bn H
	14d		" fatigues & church parade	Bn H
	15d		1 Officer & 12 OR fatigues for 15th H.A. Bde Waggon Line	Bn H
	16		"	Bn H

Army Form C. 2118.

WAR DIARY
or
INTELLIGENCE SUMMARY.
(Erase heading not required.)

Instructions regarding War Diaries and Intelligence Summaries are contained in F.S. Regs., Part II. and the Staff Manual respectively. Title pages will be prepared in manuscript.

Place	Date	Hour	Summary of Events and Information	Remarks and references to Appendices
Westenhanger	17th		10 ORs fatigue for 15th A. Bde Wagon line. 2 ORs building huts. 2 ORs Ammunition dump fatigue	
"	18th	12.0 Rs	— do —	
"	19th	12.0 Rs	— do —	
"	20th	10.0 Rs	2 ORs fatigue for 29th D.A. Hqr.	
"	21st		— do —	
"	22		— do —	
"	23		fatigues in Camp 3 ORs rejoined from School of Mortars 5th Army. Loading G.S. wagons on to train for 29 TAC & entrained for Boulleurs	
Proven	24			
Boulleurs	25		Arrived Boulleurs. Unloading wagons from train for bde & proceeded to Beaumarie.	
Beaumarie	26		Rollcall 9 am fatigue in camp Roll call 2 pm.	
"	27		— do — 11 AM Kit inspection	
"	28		Bath, Church Parade 11.15	
"	29		9 am Route march 2 pm gun & stores inspection	
"	30		Left Beaumarie & proceeded to St Léger.	
St Léger	31		Fatigues in Camp on digging gun positions	

Capt Halbot
2/Lt RFA
OC. X/29 TMB

Confidential

War Diary

of

Y/29 Trench Mortar Battery R.A.

From October 1st 1917 To October 31st 1917.

Volume No 15.

Army Form C. 2118.

WAR DIARY October 1917
INTELLIGENCE SUMMARY.
(Erase heading not required.)

Y. 29 TRENCH MORTAR BATTERY.

Instructions regarding War Diaries and Intelligence Summaries are contained in F. S. Regs., Part II. and the Staff Manual respectively. Title pages will be prepared in manuscript.

Place	Date 1917 October	Hour	Summary of Events and Information	Remarks and references to Appendices
WOFSTON BELGIUM	1		1 Man attached to D.A.C. on Transport work. 3 men attending 5th Army School of Mortars. Erecting Horse Lines & standings for 15th Brigade R.H.A. Brigade Parade 6 A.M. Erecting Horse Lines & standings for 15th Brigade R.H.A.	H.Q.B.
do	2			H.Q.B.B.
do	3		do	
	4		do	
	5th	4 A.M.	working party for 17th Brigade R.F.A. digging advanced gun positions	H.Q.B.B.
	6th	4 A.M.	do	H.Q.B.B.
	7th	4 A.M.	& carrying ammunition. 1 N.C.O & 3 men formed Brigade Guard. Working party as above for 17th Brigade R.F.A.	H.Q.B.B.
	8th	4 A.M.	do. 1 N.C.O & 3 men formed Brigade Guard. 1 Man attached to D.A.C at Truck Farm ammunition Dump.	H.Q.B.B.
	9th		Working party for 17th Brigade, carrying ammunition etc. Brigade Parade 10 A.M. Camp Fatigues etc.	H.Q.B.B.
	10th		do 1 N.C.O & 3 men Brigade Guard.	H.Q.B.B.
	11th		Brigade Parade 8.45. Erecting Horse Lines & standings for 15th Brigade R.H.A & making Road & digging drains from main road to 15th Brigade Head Quarters	H.Q.B.B.

Army Form C. 2118.

Y. 29
TRENCH MORTAR BATTERY.

WAR DIARY
or
INTELLIGENCE SUMMARY.
October 1917
(Erase heading not required.)

Instructions regarding War Diaries and Intelligence Summaries are contained in F.S. Regs., Part II. and the Staff Manual respectively. Title pages will be prepared in manuscript.

Place	Date	Hour	Summary of Events and Information	Remarks and references to Appendices
WOESTEN	1917 Oct 12th		Brigade Parade 8.45. Making Roadway & digging drains from main road to 15th Brigade Head Quarters.	T.M.B.D
"	13th		do	T.M.B.D
"	14th		Church Parade. Making Roadway & digging drains from main road to 15th Brigade Head Quarters	T.M.B.D
"	15th		Brigade Parade 8.45 do	T.M.B.D
"	16th 17th		3 men formed Brigade Guard Brigade Parade 8.45 Making Roadway etc from main road to 15 Brigade H.Q. do	1 N.B.O T.M.B.D
"	18th 19th		2 men to report to D.A. Manifean farm to erect Shelters Brigade Parade 8.45. Making Roadway from main road to 15 Brigade H.Q. do	T.M.B.D T.M.B.D
"	20th		2 men to report to D.A. for duty. 1 man to join fatigue party to build dug-out just beyond Boeshing's canal Brigade Parade 8.45 Making Roadway etc from main road to 15 Brigade H.Q. 1 N.B.O. 3 men formed Brigade Guard	T.M.B.D

Army Form C. 2118.

Y. 29
TRENCH MORTAR BATTERY.

WAR DIARY October 1917

INTELLIGENCE SUMMARY.

(Erase heading not required.)

Instructions regarding War Diaries and Intelligence Summaries are contained in F. S. Regs., Part II. and the Staff Manual respectively. Title pages will be prepared in manuscript.

Place	Date	Hour	Summary of Events and Information	Remarks and references to Appendices
WOESTEN	1917 October 21		Brigade Parade 8.45. Making Roadway etc from Main Road to 15 Bde H.Q	JHBB
"	22		do	JHBB
"	23		Brigade Parade 9.45. Cleaning up Camp &c	JHBB
"	24		do The 3 men attending 5th Army School returned to Camp. 2 men to report to D.A. for Fatigues 1 man returned to Battery from Tenth Farm Dump. Struck Camp & marched to Proven. Entrained one section of the D.A.C. & unloaded two sections of D.A.C on arriving at Boulbruis on the morning of 26th inst.	JHBB
"	25			JHBB
Couvemont	26		Marched to Billets at Couvemont.	JHBB
do	27		Brigade Parade 9.30. 1 N.C.O. 3 men formed Brigade Guard. 11 o'clock Kit Inspection. Brigade Parade 2 o'clock	JHBB
do	28		Brigade Parade 9.30. 11.15 Church Parade. Brigade Parade 2 o'clock. 5 o'clock Bathing Parade	JHBB
do	29		Brigade Parade 9.30. Route March. Gas Helmet Inspection by Gas N.C.O. from School. Inspection of Guns & Gun stores	JHBB
do	30		left Couvemont by Motor lorries arrived Patricia's Camp 4 o'clock PM	JHBB

Army Form C. 2118.

Y.29 TRENCH MORTAR BATTERY

WAR DIARY October 1917
or
INTELLIGENCE SUMMARY.
(Erase heading not required.)

Instructions regarding War Diaries and Intelligence Summaries are contained in F. S. Regs., Part II. and the Staff Manual respectively. Title pages will be prepared in manuscript.

Place	Date	Hour	Summary of Events and Information	Remarks and references to Appendices
ST LEGER FRANCE Patricia Camp	1917 October 31st	10 PM	Digging Trench Mortar Gun Positions until 6 AM next day.	

H.B.Welsh Lieut RFA
Commdg Y.29 TM Bty

Confidential

War Diary

of

Z/29 Trench Mortar Battery R.A.

From October 1st 1917. To October 31st 1917.

Volume No 15.

WAR DIARY of X/29 Medium Trench Mortar By
INTELLIGENCE SUMMARY.
(Erase heading not required.)

October 1917

Place	Date	Hour	Summary of Events and Information	Remarks and references to Appendices
Boeslen BELGIUM	Oct 1		Building horse standing for 15th Brigade R.H.A.	
	2		1 Off & 6 O.R. School of Instors 5th Army.	
	3		Digging forward position for 15 Brigade R.H.A. & 17 Brigade R.F.A.	
	4		2 O.R. attached 16 x IV Corps ammunition dump.	
	5/7			
	7		Carrying ammunition to forward field battery positions	
	8		Repitching tents and building sandbag walls around same	
	9		Fatigue around camp.	
	10		Do — Do — Do	
	11		Building horse standings for 15 Brigade R.H.A.	
	12		Do — Do — Do	
	13		Church Parade.	
	14		Building horse standing for 15 Brigade R.H.A.	
	15		Do — Do — Do	
	16		Do — Do — Do	
	17		2 O.R. to D.A.H.Q. for fatigue	
	18		Building horse standings for 15th Brigade R.H.A.	

WAR DIARY of № 29 "Medium Trench Mortar By"
or
INTELLIGENCE SUMMARY. for October, (Continued)

Army Form C. 2118.

Place	Date Oct.	Hour	Summary of Events and Information	Remarks and references to Appendices
Roeulen	19		Building horse standings for 15 Brigade R.H.A.	
"	20		Do Do	
"	21		Do Do	
"	22		Do Do	
"	23		Fatigues in camp. 10 O/R's + 50 O.R's reported from School of Mortars 5th Army.	
Roeulen	24		Loading Wagons to train for a.b. & entrained for Saulens	
Saulens FRANCE	25		Arrived & Saulens. Unloading wagons from trains for Si a.b. & proceeded to Baumecourt	
Baumecourt	26		Roll call 9AM Fatigues in Camp. 2 pm roll call	
"	27		11 AM Kit inspection 2 pm Roll call.	
"	28		8.30 Baths 11.15 Church Parade. 2 pm roll call.	
"	29		9 am Route march & pm gun drill & inspection	
"	30		Left Baumecourt & proceeded to St Leger.	
St Leger	31st		Fatigues in camp. for digging gun positions	

M Sugh Capt R.F.A
7/11/17

Confidential

War Diary

of

V/29 Heavy Trench Mortar Battery R.A.

From November 1st 1917 To November 30th 1917

Volume No 16

Army Form C. 2118.

WAR DIARY
or 7/v/29. H.T.M.B.
INTELLIGENCE SUMMARY.
(Erase heading not required.)

Place	Date	Hour	Summary of Events and Information	Remarks and references to Appendices
In the field 1st to 6 Nov.			Making 6" trench mortar positions for 3rd Division at BULLECOURT	note
"	6-11-14		1 Officer & 17 O.R's proceeded to HEUDECOURT attached to 20th Division to assist with Trench Mortar positions	note
	7th to 11th		2 Officers & 30 O.R's assist 3rd Division at BULLECOURT	note
	12th		Entrained at BAPAUME for BELLE-EGLISE marched to VILLE-SOUS-CORBIE	note
	13			
	14		Rest?	
	15th		Moved to ETRICOURT	
	16th 16th		Fatigues with 29th D.A.C.	note
	23rd		Put in 4 6" Newton trench mortars into position in MASNIERES	
	23rd		2 Officers & 25 O.R's assist on Ammunition dumps at VILLERS-PLOUICH	note
	24th to 30th		Making 9.45 Trench Mortars positions at MASNIERES	
			Entries Supervised by	
			Worrad Capt.	
			O.C. 29 H.T.M.B.	

Confidential

WK16

War Diary

of

X/29 Trench Mortar Battery. R.F.A

From:- November 1st 1917 To November 30th 1917

Volume No 16

WAR DIARY
or
INTELLIGENCE SUMMARY.
(Erase heading not required.)

Army Form C. 2118.

Instructions regarding War Diaries and Intelligence Summaries are contained in F.S. Regs., Part II. and the Staff Manual respectively. Title pages will be prepared in manuscript.

Place	Date	Hour	Summary of Events and Information	Remarks and references to Appendices
St. Ledger	1st		Attached to 16th Division, digging Dug-outs & pits for 6" Trench Howitzer.	Pleid
"	8th		Do. Do. Do.	Pleid
"	9th		Do. Do. Do.	Pleid
St. Ledger	10th		Digging Gun Pits for 2" & 6" Trench Howitzers.	Pleid
"	14		Do. Do.	Pleid
"	15th		Ammunition Fatigues & Fatigues in Camp.	Pleid
"	18		Do. Do.	Pleid
"	19		Firing 6" Trench Howitzer on barbed wire & strong point.	Pleid
"	20th		Attached 16th Division carrying ammunition for 6" Trench Howitzers	Pleid
"	21st		Do. Do. Do.	Pleid
"	22nd		Do. Do. Do.	Pleid
"	23rd		Struck Camp, removed to Etricourt. V.3. Camp. Fatigues in Camp.	Pleid
Etricourt	24		Battery in action at Manieres, with 6" Trench Howitzers	Pleid
"	25		Do. Do. Do.	Pleid
"	26		Do. Do. Do.	Pleid
"	27		½ Remainder of Bty remove to Villers-Plouich	Pleid
Villers-Bry Plouich	28/29/30		Do. Do.	Plouich Pleid

Confidential

War Diary

of

Y/29 Trench Mortar Battery RA

From :- November 1st 1917 To November 30th 1917.

Volume No 16.

WAR DIARY or INTELLIGENCE SUMMARY

Army Form C. 2118.

Unit: 1/29 TMB
Month: November 1917

Place	Date	Hour	Summary of Events and Information	Remarks and references to Appendices
Patricia's Camp	1917 Nov 1		Digging 6" Trench Mortar Gun Positions & Dug-outs for 16 Div TMBs	WBB
	2		do	WBB
	3		do	WBB
	4		do	WBB
	5		do	WBB
	6		do	WBB
	7		do	2 men for Guard WBB
	8		do	1 man for Guard WBB
	9		do	2 men " " WBB
	10		do	1 man " " WBB
	11		Digging two 6" Trench Mortar Gun Positions &c for our Battery	2 men " " WBB
	12		do	WBB
	13		do	WBB
	14		do	WBB
	15		do	WBB
	16		do & placing Guns in Action	WBB

WAR DIARY

Army Form C. 2118

November 1917

INTELLIGENCE SUMMARY

(Erase heading not required.)

Place	Date	Hour	Summary of Events and Information	Remarks and references to Appendices
	1917			
Patricia Camp	Nov 17		Carrying 6" Trench Mortar Ammunition to Gun Positions	JWBB
	18		do	JWBB
			No 1 Gun T 6 rounds from No 2 Gun	JWBB
	19		Carrying Ammunition & fired 47 rounds from No 1 Gun T 19 rounds from No 2 Gun	JWBB
	20		Carrying 6" Trench Mortar Ammunition for 16 Divn'l T.M. Bty's	JWBB
	21		do	JWBB
	22		do	JWBB
	23		Left Patricia Camp & proceeded to Etricourt to 39th D.A.C.	JWBB
	24		1 Officer & 14 Men left Etricourt for Manieres & placed two 6" Trench Mortar Guns in Action	JWBB
Etricourt			With two Guns the Battery fired 64 rounds	JWBB
	25		do	JWBB
	26		do 75 rounds	JWBB
	27		39 rounds T the remainder of the Battery left Etricourt & proceeded to Villers-Plouich. 3 min. for'nd Batteries in Reserve	JWBB
Villers-Plouich	28		The Battery fired 94 rounds. 1 Man carrying returns to men in line	JWBB

WAR DIARY November 1914
INTELLIGENCE SUMMARY.

Army Form C. 2118.

Place	Date	Hour	Summary of Events and Information	Remarks and references to Appendices
Villers-Plouich	1914 Nov 29 30		The Battery fire 7 rounds No 4 Gun " " "	2 NBS H.B.Beker Lieut RFA Commdg V/29 TMBy

Confidential

War Diary

of

Z/29 Trench Mortar Battery R.A.

From:- November 1st 1917 to November 30th 1917

Volume No 16.

WAR DIARY of 29 Medium Trench Mortar Bty

INTELLIGENCE SUMMARY.
(Erase heading not required.)

for November 1917

Place	Date	Hour	Summary of Events and Information	Remarks and references to Appendices
at Sedyn	1st–9th		Making positions for 6" Newton trench mortars, for 16th Division	nil.
do	10th		Rigging positions for 2" & 6" French mortars	nil.
do	10th–14th		Carrying ammunition up to positions	nil.
do	15th–18th		Firing 6" Newton on barbed wire & strongpoints south of FONTAINE.	nil.
do	19th		Carrying ammunition 6" Newton for 16th Division	nil.
do	20th–22nd		Moved to Equancourt V's camp, 6" section in action at MASNIERES. two detachments	nil.
Equancourt	23			nil.
	24/27		Remainder of Battery removed to Villers Plouich	nil.
	27. 28/30		In action at MASNIERES	nil.

M. Hay Lieut R.F.A.
O.C. T.M.B.
Z 6 Z.

X29. Trench Mortar Battery

WAR DIARY
or
INTELLIGENCE SUMMARY.
(Erase heading not required.)

Army Form C. 2118.

December 1917.

Place	Date	Hour	Summary of Events and Information	Remarks and references to Appendices
In the Field	1st.		Battery returned out of action Masnieres OC & 16 O.R's attacked towards/ defense of MASNIERES	OC Killed 15 att
	2nd 3rd to 10th		" at Etricourt Battery attached to D.A.C. for fatigues	2att
	13th		Battery left Etricourt for Trevines	1att
	14th 15th		Battery resting at Trevines	1att
	16th		Battery left Trevines for Achiens.	1att
	17th to 20th		Battery attached to D.A.C. for fatigues	1att Battn
	21st		Battery entrained at Verennes arriving at Hoodin,	1att
	23rd		Battery marched from Hoodin to Equinia aint	1att
	24th		Battery marched from Equinia out to Maresquel.	1att
	25th		Battery at Maresquel.	1att
	26th 27th 28th 29th 30th 31st		Battery training. Parade drill, Gymnastics etc. Also 1 OR's attend Lewis Gun Course. Battn. also including training in the use of bombs.	6att

B. Mullins,
Lieut R.F.A.
o/c X29 Trench Mortar Battery

Confidential

War Diary

of

V/29 Heavy Trench Mortar Battery T.P.A.

From: December 1st 1917. To: December 31st 1917.

Volume No. 17.

Army Form C. 2118.

WAR DIARY
of 29 H.T.M.B
INTELLIGENCE SUMMARY.
(Erase heading not required.)

Instructions regarding War Diaries and Intelligence Summaries are contained in F.S. Regs., Part II. and the Staff Manual respectively. Title pages will be prepared in manuscript.

Place	Date	Hour	Summary of Events and Information	Remarks and references to Appendices
In the Field	Dec'y 1st		Evacuated MASNIERES for Keem L Murry N & Wells a missing	
	2nd to 12th		Returned to ETRICOURT. Fatigues with 29th D.A.C. Horse lines	
	13th		1 Officer & 15 O.R. proceeded to 5th Army School of Mortars to undergo a course of instruction.	
	14th		Moved to TREUX.	
	17th		Moved to ACHEUX	
	18th & 19th		Physical exercise & Fatigues	
	20th			
	21st		Entrained at VERENNES for MARESQUEL	
	23rd		Detrained at HESDIN & marched to EQUEMICOURT	
	24th		Moved to MARESQUEL	
	25th to 31st		Physical exercise & instruction in bombing, & the use of Lewis Machine gun	

J.B.Archer
Lieut R.F.A.

Confidential

War Diary

of

Y/29 Trench Mortar Battery. T.P.A.

From: December 1st 1917 To. December 31st 1917.

Volume No. 17.

WAR DIARY December 1914
of Y/29 TMB
INTELLIGENCE SUMMARY.

Army Form C. 2118.

Place	Date	Hour	Summary of Events and Information	Remarks and references to Appendices
Ebecourt	Dec 1/7 1		Battery in action Mesnières. Fired 100 rounds working in conjunction with Z Bty.	MBB
	2		Left Mesnières on the night of the first & arrived at Headquarters D.A.C. at Ebecourt on the morning of the second.	MBB
	3		Camp fatigues. Cleaning up & kit Inspection. Brigade Parades 9 o'clock & 2 o'clock. Fatigues for D.A.C.	MBB
	4		Brigade Parades 9 o'clock & 2 o'clock. Fatigues for D.A.C. Inspection of Guns & Gun Stores.	MBB
	5		Brigade Parades 9 AM & 2 PM. Fatigues for D.A.C.	MBB
	6		do. Sergeant & 4 men for Picquet.	MBB
	7		do.	MBB
	8		do. Sergeant & 4 men for Picquet.	MBB
	9		do. Church Parade.	MBB
	10		Brigade Parades 9 AM & 2 PM. Fatigues for D.A.C.	MBB
	11			
	12			

WAR DIARY or INTELLIGENCE SUMMARY

Army Form C. 2118.

December 1/17

Place	Date	Hour	Summary of Events and Information	Remarks and references to Appendices
Bricourt	Dec/17 13		Brigade Parade 9 A.M. 2 P.M. Fatigues for D.A.C. 1 N.C.O. 3 men for guard on Ammunition Dump.	24BB
	14		Left Bricourt & marched to Treux	24BB
Treux	15		Cleaning up of kit etc	24BB
	16		Brigade Church Parade	24BB
	17		Left Treux & marched to Achiet	24BB
Achiet	18		Physical Training. Fatigues for D.A.C.	24BB
	19		do	
	20			24BB
	21		Left Achiet & marched to Vecemvers & entrained	24BB
	22			
	23		Arrived at Heaben & detrained & marched to Equancourt	24BB
Equancourt	24		Left Equancourt & marched to Moraguel	24BB
Moraguel	25		Brigade Parade 10 P.M.	24BB
	26		do	24BB

WAR DIARY - December / 17
or
INTELLIGENCE SUMMARY.
(Erase heading not required.)

Army Form C. 2118.

Place	Date	Hour	Summary of Events and Information	Remarks and references to Appendices
Montagueil	Dec/17			
	27	7.30 AM	Physical Training 9.30 Brigade Parade & Marching Drill 2 P.M Brigade Parade & Physical Training	WBB
	28	7.30 AM	Physical Training. 9.30 P.M. Brigade Parade. Instruction on Bomb Throwing & Firing Rifle Grenade. 1 P.M. Brigade Parade Marched to Braquemville for Instruction on Lewis Gun. 2 P.M. Physical Training	WBB
	29			
	30			
	30		for remainder of Battery. On the 30th See Church Parade for R.B. at 10 P.M	

W.B.B.Oakey
Lieut. R.F.A
Comndg 4/29 T.M.Bty.

Confidential

War Diary

of

Z/29 Trench Mortar Battery. T.P.A.

From: December 1st 1917. To December 31st 1917.

Volume No. 17.

Army Form C. 2118.

WAR DIARY
of
INTELLIGENCE SUMMARY.
(Erase heading not required.)

Y/29 T.M. B/y.
(December).

Instructions regarding War Diaries and Intelligence Summaries are contained in F. S. Regs., Part II. and the Staff Manual respectively. Title pages will be prepared in manuscript.

Place	Date	Hour	Summary of Events and Information	Remarks and references to Appendices
In Line	1st		Battery in action at Jasmikal. Enemy advanced. Barrage put up in conjunction with Y.29 when about 100 Rds were fired.	M/1
	2nd		Ordered to evacuate.	M/1
	3rd		Battery at Elincourt.	M/1
Field	4th			M/1
	5th			
	6th			
	7th			
	8th		Attached to 29th D.A.C. for fatigues, assisting in stables	M/8
	9th			
	10th			
	11th			
	12th			
	13th		Battery left Elincourt for Freux. (Marched 25 miles)	M/1
	14th		Resting at Freux.	M/1
	15th		Left Freux marched to Acheux (8 miles)	M/1
	16th		Battery at Acheux, attached to 29th D.A.C. for fatigues (stables etc).	M/1
	17th			M/1
	18th			M/1
	19th			M/1
	20th			M/1
	21st		Left Acheux & entrained at Vannerins arriving at Hesdin 22/12/17.	M/1
	22nd			M/1
	23rd		Marched from Hesdin to Eguinecourt (6 miles)	M/1
	24th			M/1
	25th		Marched from Eguinecourt to Maresquel. (1½ miles).	M/1
	26th		Battery at Maresquel. Parade 9.30 a.m.	M/1
	27th		Parade 7.30 a.m. Physical drill. 9.30 a.m. Marching drill. 2.0 p.m. Marching drill.	M/1
	28th			M/1
	29th			M/1
	30th		Parade 7.30 a.m. Physical drill. 9.30 a.m. Hand Grenade practice. 2.0 p.m. 4 ORs Lewis Gun course.	M/1
	31st			M/1

Lieut. R.F.A.
O/c Y/29 Trench Mortar Bty

Confidential

— War Diary —

of

V/29 Heavy Trench Mortar Battery. R.A.

From: January 1st 1918 To: January 31st 1918

Volume No. 18.

Army Form C. 2118.

WAR DIARY
of OF V/29 HTMB
INTELLIGENCE SUMMARY.
(Erase heading not required.)

Place	Date	Hour	Summary of Events and Information	Remarks and references to Appendices
In the Field	Jan 1st to 3rd		Physical exercise, Bombing & recoil, drill, gun practice.	
	3rd			
	4th		Ordered for a course to the Army T.M. School.	
	5th		Entrained at MARQUISE for VAUX-EN-AMIENOIS for a course of instructions on Heavy Trench Mortars	
	6th			
	10th		Finishing a course at L.C.Army T.M. School	
	14th		Entrained at AMIENS for POPERINGHE	
	22nd		Moved to ST-JEAN	
	23rd		One Officer & 29 O.R. attached to 252 Tunnelling Company R.E. for work	
			Remainder of Battery on salvage work at GRAVENSTAFEL	
	31st			

Charles Loutrec
O.C. V/29 H.T.M.B.

Confidential

War Diary

of

X/29 Trench Mortar Battery. R.A.

From: January 1st 1918 To: January 31st 1918

Volume No. 18

January 1918. X.29. T.M.B. WAR DIARY

Army Form C. 2118.

INTELLIGENCE SUMMARY.

(Erase heading not required.)

Instructions regarding War Diaries and Intelligence Summaries are contained in F. S. Regs., Part II. and the Staff Manual respectively. Title pages will be prepared in manuscript.

Place	Date	Hour	Summary of Events and Information	Remarks and references to Appendices
1918	Jany 1		Battery Training at Maresquel.	B.S.H
"	2			
"	3		Battery leave Maresquel for Merck St Lievin,	B.S.H
"	4			
"	5			
"	6 to 10		Battery Training at Merck St Lievin.	B.S.H
"			Battery leave Merck St Lievin for En Eyppe,	
"	11		En Eyppe.	B.S.H
"	12		" for Oudezeele	B.S.H
"	13		" Oudezeele for Poperinghe	B.S.H
"	14 to 18		Battery Training at Poperinghe	B.S.H
"	19		Battery leave Poperinghe for Vlamertinghe	B.S.H
"	20 to 23		Battery preparing positions Belle Vue,	B.S.H
"	24 to 27		Battery resting at Vlamertinghe	B.S.H
"	28 to 31		Battery preparing forward positions Hanebeke Ridge,	B.S.H

Pan Hulhet Lt.
o/c X 29. T.M.B.

Confidential

~~ War Diary ~~

of

Y/29 Trench Mortar Battery. R.A.

From: January 1st 1918: To: January 31st 1918

Volume No. 18

WAR DIARY
or
INTELLIGENCE SUMMARY.

Army Form C. 2118.

January 1918.

Place	Date	Hour	Summary of Events and Information	Remarks and references to Appendices
Marsoquel	1918 Jan 1		Brigade Parade 9.30 Marching Drill. Instruction on Mills Bombs & Rifle Grenades. 1.30 Marched to Braconville for Instruction on Lewis Machine Gun. Physical Instruction for remainder of Battery.	W3B
	2nd	7.30	Physical Instruction. Parade 9.30 Machine Drill Instruction on Mills Bomb & Rifle Grenades. 1.30 Instruction on Lewis Gun at Braconville. Physical Instruction.	W3B
	3/1		do	W3B
	4/1		No Lewis Gun School on this date	W3B
Meth H Sern	5/1		Left Marsoquel & proceeded to Meth H Sern by Motor Lorries.	W3B
	6	9.30 9.15	Brigade Parade & Inspection 2 o'clock Brigade Parade. R.C.'s Church Parade 9.30 C of E's Church Parade	W3B
	7	7.30	Physical Instruction 9.30 Brigade Parade. Gun Drill. 2 o'clock Marching Drill & Gun Drill	W3B
	8		do	W3B
	9	7.30	Physical Instruction 9.30 Parade & Route March. 2 o'clock Gun Drill Lorry & Instruction on Mop reading	W3B
	10	7.30	Physical Training. 9.30 Parade. Gun Drill. 2 o'clock Gun Drill	W3B

Army Form C. 2118.

WAR DIARY
or
INTELLIGENCE SUMMARY.
(Erase heading not required.)

Instructions regarding War Diaries and Intelligence Summaries are contained in F.S. Regs., Part II. and the Staff Manual respectively. Title pages will be prepared in manuscript.

Place	Date	Hour	Summary of Events and Information	Remarks and references to Appendices
Mata-fr-Serin	Jan 1918 11		Left Mata fr Serin & marched to Renescure	ASR
	12		Marched from Renescure to Oudenzeele	ASR
	13		Left Oudenzeele & marched to Poperinghe	ASR
Poperinghe	14	9.30	Brigade Parade. Inspection of Billets. 2 o'clock Parade	ASR
	15	8.45	Battery Parade. Inspection of Kit to 9.15 Bathing Parade. Inspection of Billets. 2 o'clock Gas Helmet Drill	ASR
	16		9 o'clock Battery Parade. Gas Helmet Drill. Billet Inspection 2 o'clock Parade Gun Laying with Gas Masks on	ASR
	17		9 o'clock Parade. Gas Helmet Drill. Billet Inspection 2 o'clock Parade Gun Drill & Laying	ASR
	18		9 o'clock Brigade Route March. Billet Inspection. 2 o'clock Parade Gun Drill. 1 man proceded on Lewis Gun Course	ASR
	19		Left Poperinghe & marched to Dhameringhe	ASR
Dhameringhe	20		Five men left for Instruction at 4th Army School of Mortars	ASR
	21		Cleaning Kit & Billet Inspection	ASR
	22		Battery proceded in the line & relieved X Battery Digging Positions etc	ASR

WAR DIARY
or
INTELLIGENCE SUMMARY.
(Erase heading not required.)

Army Form C. 2118.

Place	Date	Hour	Summary of Events and Information	Remarks and references to Appendices
Mauetruyte	1918 Jan 23		Battery in line Tagging Gun Positions &c	WBB
	24		do	WBB
	25		Battery relieved by Z 29.Bty	WBB
	26		Cleaning up kit etc	WBB
	27		Bathing Parade. Billet Inspection	WBB
	28		Billet Inspection	WBB
	29	2.30 PM	Ten men carried material for Gun Pits etc to forward positions	WBB
	30	2.30 AM	do	WBB
	31		9.30 Battery Parade. Billet Inspection. 2 o'clock Parade. Gun laying.	WBB

W.B.Boley
Lieut R.F.A.
Commdg Y/29 T M Bty.

Confidential

— War Diary —

of

Z/29 Trench Mortar Battery. R.A.

From: January 1st 1918 To: January 31st 1918

Volume No 18

WAR DIARY
or
INTELLIGENCE SUMMARY.
(Erase heading not required.)

Army Form C. 2118.

T/29 Trench Mortar Battery
January

Place	Date	Hour	Summary of Events and Information	Remarks and references to Appendices
MARESQUES	1st		Parades 7.30am Physical Drill. 9.30am Hand Grenade Practice. 2.0pm Lewis Gun Course	JMS
	2nd			
	3rd		Parades 7.30am Physical Drill. 9.30am Marching Drill. 2.0pm Marching Drill.	JMS
	4th		Battery left MARESQUES and proceeded to MERCK ST KIEVIN by lorries.	JMS
	5th		Cleaning billets and guns etc	
MERCK ST KIEVIN	6th			
	7th			
	8th		Parades 7.30am Physical Drill. 9.30am Gun Drill. 2.0pm Marching Drill	JMS
	9th			
RENESCURE	10th		Battery left MERCK ST KIEVIN and marched to RENESCURE	JMS
	11th		Battery left RENESCURE and marched to OUDEZEELE	JMS
OUDEZEELE	12th		Battery left OUDEZEELE and marched to POPERINGHE.	JMS
POPERINGHE	13th		Cleaning billets, guns etc.	
	14th		9.0am Gas-mask Inspection. 2.0pm Gun Drill.	JMS
	15th		9.0am Bathing Parade. 2.0pm Gun Drill	JMS
	16th		9.0am Gas mask Inspection 2.0pm Gun Drill.	JMS
	17th		Gun Drill 9am. 1.30pm Gas test at Gas Chamber.	JMS
	18th		Battery left POPERINGHE and marching to VLAMERTINGHE	JMS
VLAMERTINGHE	19th			
	20th		Officers & 4 O.R's proceeding to II Army Trench Mortar School	
WIEJLE CORNER	21st		W.R.S proceeded to WIEJSE CORNER attached to 250 R.E.	JMS
	22nd		Issuing 250 R.E Coy tunnelling	JMS
VLAMERTINGHE	23rd		Battery left WIEJSE CORNER and returned to VLAMERTINGHE	JMS
	24th		Bathing Parade	JMS
			Battery Resting	JMS

WAR DIARY "Z" 29 T.M.B (Cont'd)

Army Form C. 2118.

Place	Date	Hour	Summary of Events and Information	Remarks and references to Appendices
VLAMERTINGHE	25th	2.30am	Battery proceeded to BELLEVUE to relieve Y 29 T.M.B. J.McP.	
BELLEVUE	25th		carrying ammunition to Reserve gun positions. J.McP.	
	26th		Obtaining ammunition nets for 16.2 gun pits. J.McP.	
	27th		Battery proceeded forward to make advanced gun positions. J.McP.	
	28th	4.0am	X 29 T.M.B. arrived at BELLEVUE J.McP.	
	28th		Both batteries carrying material to advanced positions. J.McP.	
VLAMERTINGHE	29th	12 noon	Z 29 T.M.B proceeded to VLAMERTINGHE J.McP.	
	29th		Battery Parade J.McP.	
	30th	2.30am	2.O.R's proceeded to BELLEVUE carrying material to advanced gun pits. J.McP.	
	30th	2.30am	2.O.R's proceeded to BELLEVUE carrying gun beds to advanced positions	
	31st		Battery Resting. J.McP	

J. McPhail
Lieut. R.F.A
i/c Z/29 Trench Mortar Battery.

Confidential

War Diary

of

X/29 Trench Mortar Battery. R.A.

From: February 1st 1918: To February 28th 1918

Volume No. 19

WAR DIARY
or
INTELLIGENCE SUMMARY.

(Erase heading not required.)

X/29 T.M. B'y. Army Form C. 2118.
(February)

Place	Date	Hour	Summary of Events and Information	Remarks and references to Appendices
VLAMERTINGHE	1st to 2nd		Battery resting	
"	3rd	10 am	W.O.R'S proceeded to I Army T.M. School	
"	4th		Re-organisation of Trench Mortar Batteries. Personnel of Bg. T.M.B. transferred to X/29 T.M.B. completed by 20 Officers & 6 O.R's from X°/29.	
St. Jean	4th		Travelling Jn. 250 R.l.'s Solinguey.	
"	10th 12th			
St. Jean	13th		Battery proceeded to POPERINGHE and took over billets from 10th 8th Divisional Trench Mortar H.Q'S Signalling School	
POPERINGHE	14th		Parade 10-11am Inspection Parade 2-3pm Whitling day.	
"	17th		12. OR's at YPRES Fatigues	
"	18th		Ditto	
"	19th		2 Officers & 40. OR's proceeded to the Army T.M. School.	
"	20th		Parade 9.30am Gas Mask Inspection	
"	21st			
"	28th		50rs at YPRES Fatigues.	

O/c X.29 T.M. B'y.

Confidential

── War Diary ──

of

Y/29 Trench Mortar Battery. R.A.

From: February 1st 1918: To February 28th 1918

Volume No. 19.

Army Form C. 2118.

WAR DIARY
or
INTELLIGENCE SUMMARY.
(Erase heading not required.)

Y29 T.M. Battery
February 17

Place	Date	Hour	Summary of Events and Information	Remarks and references to Appendices
Belle Vue	1st		Lieut Bilbu + 9 ORs making advanced gun positions.	
Vlamertinghe	1st		Remainder of battery resting	
"	2nd		" " " "	
"	3rd		Ditto. 1 Officer + 14 ORs relieved to battery from II Army T.M. School	
"	3rd		16 ORs proceeded to II Army T.M. School	
"	4th		Remainder of battery resting. Reinforcements of T.M. batteries posted to Y29 T.M.B. & X29 T.M.B. transferred to Y29 T.M.B.	
"	5th		Ditto	
"	5th		Capt Guy + 12 ORs proceeded to Belle Vue to relieve Lieut Bilbu +	
Belle Vue	5th		Lieut Bilbu + 9 ORs proceeded to Vlamertinghe	
"	6th		Capt Guy + 12 ORs making advanced gun positions	
"	7th		Remainder of battery resting	
Vlamertinghe	6th		" " " "	
"	7th			
Belle Vue	8th		Capt Guy recalled on Brigade's own employment	
"	8th		Capt Guy wounded and sent to hospital	
Vlamertinghe	9th		Lieut Bilbu + 13 ORs proceeded to Belle Vue	
Belle Vue	9th		Firing on enemy's gun emplacements	
"	10th		Ditto	

WAR DIARY or INTELLIGENCE SUMMARY

Army Form C. 2118.

Y.29 T.M. B'y (Contd) February.

Place	Date	Hour	Summary of Events and Information	Remarks and references to Appendices
RALLE VOE	11th		Carrying ammunition to advanced gun positions	Afm
"	12th		Firing on Enemy's Gun emplacements	Afm
"	13th		Battery manned by 8th Devonshires trench mortars	Afm
VLAMERTINGHE	14th		Battery proceeded to POPERINGHE and took over billets from 8th Divison.	Afm
POPERINGHE	15th		Battery resting, cleaning guns etc.	Afm
"	16th		Parade 9 am. Gas mask inspection. Serade 2 pm. Gun Drill inspection.	Afm
"	17th		3 Officers & 23 O.R's proceeded to YPRES loading stores	Afm
"	18th		Ditto	Afm
"	19th		Ditto	Afm
"	20th		2 Officers & 0 O.R's proceeded to T.M. Army T.M. School 16 O.R's returned to battery from II Army T.M. school	Afm
"	21st		1 Officer & 24 O.R's proceeded YPRES loading stores	Afm
"	22nd		Ditto	Afm
"	23rd			

WAR DIARY
or
INTELLIGENCE SUMMARY.
(Erase heading not required.)

Army Form C. 2118.

Y 29 T.M. Bty (Cork's) (February.)

Place	Date	Hour	Summary of Events and Information	Remarks and references to Appendices
POPERINGHE	24/2/17		1 Officer & 24 O.R.S proceeded to YPRES loading stores	AJM
"	26/2/17		1 Officer & 24 O.R.S proceeded to YPRES loading stores	AJM
"	27/2/17		Lewis Gun drill with Gas helmets.	AJM
"	28/2/17			

A.J. Mulley
2nd Lieut
O/C Y.29 T.M.Bty.

Confidential

War Diary

of

Z/29 Trench Mortar Battery. R.A.

From: February 1st 1918 To February 28th 1918

Volume No. 19

Vol 19

WAR DIARY or INTELLIGENCE SUMMARY

Army Form C. 2118.

X/39 T.M. Battery (February).

(Erase heading not required.)

Place	Date	Hour	Summary of Events and Information	Remarks and references to Appendices
WARLUS ARTIGNY	1st		Nothing doing	M.S.
BERLES VILLE	1st		2 O.R's arrived X/39 T.M.B working advanced gun positions	M.S.
WARLUS TONIGHT	2nd		Battery refitting	M.S.
" "	3rd		2 O.R's proceeded to II Army T.M School	M.S.
" "	4th		Reorganisation of Trench Mortar Batteries carried out in X/39 T.M.B	M.S.
			Transferred to X/39 T.M Battery	

J.M. Cope 2nd Lieut.
o/c X/39 Trench Mortar Batt.

Confidential

War Diary

of

V/29 Heavy Trench Mortar Battery. R.A.

From: February 1st 1918 To: February 28th 1918

Volume No. 19

WAR DIARY
or
INTELLIGENCE SUMMARY.
(Erase heading not required.)

V/29 T.M. Bty. February. Army Form C. 2118.

Place	Date	Hour	Summary of Events and Information	Remarks and references to Appendices
ST JEAN	1st	9 f.	Searching for 250 R.G.S. Gunner Renshaw killed in action	M.S.
	10.3.17		Gunner's funeral. Guns etc Salvaging.	
	7th	9.30am	Re-organisation of Trench Mortar Batteries. Personnel of V/29 R.F.A. transferred to X/29 T.M.By. R.G.A. Personnel transferred to 8th Corps Artillery	M.S.

M.S.
2/Lieut TMA
for OC V/29 HTMB

Vol 20

Confidential

War Diary

of

X/29. T.M.B. R.A.

from
March 1st 1918 to March 31st 1918

Volume 20.

Army Form C. 2118.

WAR DIARY
or
INTELLIGENCE SUMMARY. X 29 T.M. Battery.
(Erase heading not required.)
(MARCH)

Instructions regarding War Diaries and Intelligence Summaries are contained in F.S. Regs., Part II. and the Staff Manual respectively. Title pages will be prepared in manuscript.

Place	Date	Hour	Summary of Events and Information	Remarks and references to Appendices
POPERINGHE	1st		2 Officers & 40 ORs at IV Army School of Mortars	A13
"	"		D.T.M.O. & 1 OR at II Army School of Mortars. 4 ORs at Signal School	A13
"	"	9.30AM	Remainder of Battery Brush Foligues YPRES	A13
"	"	4.0 PM	Gun Drill with Gas Helmets	A13
"	2nd		2 Officers & 40 ORs at IV Army School of Mortars	A13
"	"		D.T.M.O & 1 OR at II Army School of Mortars. 4 ORs at Signal School	A13
"	"	9.30AM	Remainder of Battery Brush Foligues YPRES	A13
"	3rd		Ditto	A13
"	4th		Ditto	A13
"	5th		Ditto	A13
"	6th		Ditto	A13
"	7th		2 Officers & 40 ORs at IV Army School of Mortars. D.T.M.O & 1 OR at II Army School of Mortars	A13
"	"		2 Officers & 3 ORs proceeded to ST JEAN to take over bullets from 8th Div T.M's	A13
"	"		4 ORs at Signal School	A13

Army Form C. 2118.

WAR DIARY
or
INTELLIGENCE SUMMARY. X 29 T.M Battery
(Erase heading not required.) (MARCH)

Place	Date	Hour	Summary of Events and Information	Remarks and references to Appendices
POPERINGHE	8TH		2 Officers + 100 O.R.s at IV Army School of Mortars. H.O.R. Signal School.	A/3
"	"		D.T.M.O. + 1 O.R. returned from IV Army School of Mortars	A/3
"	"		2 Officers & 30 O.R.s proceed with Y Bty to take over Gun Position from 8th Div. T.M.B	A/3
"	"		2nd Lt J.M. Gough killed in action and 1 O.R. wounded and taken to Hospital.	A/3
"	"		Remainder of Battery moved to VLAMERTINGHE and took over billets.	A/3
"	"		from 8th Div. T.M.B. Pay issued to Battery.	A/3
VLAMERTINGHE	9TH		2 Officers + 40 O.R.s travelling from T.M. School. H.O.R. ol Signal School.	A/3
"	"		Remainder of Battery Goo Helmet inspection	A/3
"	10TH		2 Officers + 40 O.R. travelling from T.M. School H O.R.s Signal School	A/3
"	"		Remainder of Battery left VLAMERTINGHE for camp near ST JEAN	A/3
"	"		2 O.R. relieved from firing line	A/3
ST. JEAN	11TH		2 Officers + O O.R. travelling from T.M. School. H O.R.s Signal School	A/3
"	"		Remainder of Battery resting	A/3

Army Form C. 2118.

WAR DIARY
or
INTELLIGENCE SUMMARY. X29 T.M. Battery
(MARCH)
(Erase heading not required.)

Instructions regarding War Diaries and Intelligence Summaries are contained in F. S. Regs., Part II. and the Staff Manual respectively. Title pages will be prepared in manuscript.

Place	Date	Hour	Summary of Events and Information	Remarks and references to Appendices
ST JEAN	12TH		2 Officers & 40 O.R's arrived at POPERINGHE from IV Army School of Mortars	LV3
"	"		4 O.R's at Signal School	LV3
"	"		Remainder of Battery resting	LV3
"	13TH		2 Officers & 40 O.R's arrived in Camp. Men ST. JEAN. 4 O.R's at Signal School	LV3
ST. JEAN	"		Remainder of Battery resting	LV3
BELLE.VUE.	14TH	9.45 A.M.	1 Officer. 36 O.R's carrying party to Gun position	LV3
ST JEAN	"		Remainder of Battery resting. 4 O.R's Signal School	LV3
BELLE VUE	15TH	7.0 A.M.	12 O.R's Clearing party Gun position. 4 O.R's Signal School	LV3
ST JEAN	"		Pay issued to Battery. Remainder of Battery resting.	LV3
BELLE.VUE.	16TH	3.45 A.M	2 Officers 16 O.R's relieved Y Bty. 4 O.R's Signal School	LV3
"	"		Remainder of Battery carrying party. 50 rounds fired on Enemy Trenches & emplacements	LV3
WIELTJE	"	10.0 P.M.	2 O.R's Loading party at OXFORD DUMP	LV3
BELLE VUE	17TH	4.0 A.M.	12 O.R's carrying party. 20 rounds fired on Enemy Trench Line & Machine Gun emplacements	LV3
ST JEAN	"		4 O.R's Signal School. 1 O.R Gas School VIII Corps.	LV3
"	"		2/Lt Gall Vanwylenburg posted to X29 T.M.B from Y29 T.M.B.	LV3

Army Form C. 2118.

WAR DIARY
or
INTELLIGENCE SUMMARY. X 29 T.M. Battery
(MARCH)
(Erase heading not required.)

Instructions regarding War Diaries and Intelligence Summaries are contained in F. S. Regs., Part II. and the Staff Manual respectively. Title pages will be prepared in manuscript.

Place	Date	Hour	Summary of Events and Information	Remarks and references to Appendices
BELLE VUE	18TH		2 Officers and 16 ORs at Gun positions. 20 rounds fired on Enemy Machine Gun and	A13
" "	" "		tunnel mortar emplacements.	A13
" "	" "		4 ORs at Signal School. 1 OR at VIII Corps Gas School. Remainder of Battery resting.	A13
ST JEAN	" "		Camp hearty shelled all day.	A13
BELLE VUE	19TH	3.30 AM	4 ORs carrying party. 20 rounds fired on Enemy Machine Gun and Mortar emplacements.	A13
" "	" "		4 ORs Signal School. 1 OR VIII Corps Gas School.	A13
BELLE VUE	20TH		14 ORs carrying party. 1 NCO wounded and taken to Hospital.	A13
" "	" "		2 Officers 16 ORs relieved by Y Battery at Gun position.	A13
ST JEAN	" "		4 ORs Signal School. 1 OR VIII Corps Gas School. Remainder of Battery resting.	A13
" "	21st		Battery resting. 4 ORs Signal School 1 OR VIII Corps Gas School.	A13
" "	" "	10.00 AM	Inspection of Gas Helmets.	A13
BELLE VUE	22nd	6.0 PM	3 ORs unloading party.	A13
ST JEAN	" "		Remainder of Battery resting. 4 ORs Signal School. 1 OR VIII Corps Gas School.	A13
BELLE VUE	23rd	9.30 AM	15 ORs carrying party.	A13
			Remainder of Battery resting. 4 ORs Signal School.	A13

Army Form C. 2118.

WAR DIARY
or
INTELLIGENCE SUMMARY. X 29 T.M. Battery
(Erase heading not required.) (MARCH)

Instructions regarding War Diaries and Intelligence Summaries are contained in F.S. Regs., Part II. and the Staff Manual respectively. Title pages will be prepared in manuscript.

Place	Date	Hour	Summary of Events and Information	Remarks and references to Appendices
BELLEVUE	24TH	3.30 AM	2 Officers 15 O.R's relieved Y Battery at Gun Position. 3 rounds fired on Enemy machine Gun and Trench Mortar emplacement from VALOUR FARM Gun position.	ℓ/3
LARMKEET	— —	5.0 PM	2 O.R's sent loading party	ℓ/3
ST JEHAN	— —		Remainder of Battery resting, 4 O.R's Signal School, 1 Officer + 2 O.R's proceeded	ℓ/3
— ". —	— —		to II Corps T.M. School	ℓ/3
Alt 28 D13 F80	25TH		4 O.R's making position for Anti Tank Gun	ℓ/3
BELLE VUE	— —	8.30 AM	8 O.R's carrying party. 1 O.R Guide for working party with material. 3 rounds fired on Enemy Machine Gun and Signal Mortar emplacement from VALOUR FARM Gun position.	ℓ/3
ST JEHAN	— —		4 O.R's Signal School 1 Officer 2 O.R's II Corps T.M School	ℓ/3
— ". —	— —		Remainder of Battery resting	ℓ/3
PASSCHENDAELE	26TH		1 Mortar mounted in position. 6 rounds fired on Enemy trench lines and	ℓ/3
— ". —	— —		emp'lacement from VALOUR FARM position.	ℓ/3
SPREE FARM	— —		4 O.R's Guarding anti-aircraft Gun position for two days. Held Battery Positions	ℓ/3
ST JEHAN	— —		4 O.R's at Signal School. 1 Officer + 2 O.R. return again II Army T.M School	ℓ/3
— ". —	— —		Remainder of Battery resting.	ℓ/3

WAR DIARY
INTELLIGENCE SUMMARY. X.29 T.M Battery
(MARCH)
(Erase heading not required.)

Army Form C. 2118.

Instructions regarding War Diaries and Intelligence Summaries are contained in F.S. Regs., Part II. and the Staff Manual respectively. Title pages will be prepared in manuscript.

Place	Date	Hour	Summary of Events and Information	Remarks and references to Appendices
PASSCHENDAELE	27TH		1 Mule's mounted in position, 6 recruits joined, Enemy shell-fire and enemy casualties from VALOUR FARM position	AV3
—	—	—		AV3
BELLEVUE	—	3.30 AM	H OR's carrying party	AV3
ST JEAN	—	—	Remainder of Battery resting, H OR at Signal School	AV3
BELLEVUE	28TH		2 Officers 16 OR's relieved by Y Battery at Gun position	AV3
—	—	6.30 PM	5 OR's evacuating party, Lieut. B.B. Bilston wounded	AV3
ST JEAN	—		Remainder of Battery resting, H OR at Signal School	AV3
Sht.28 D13.F80	29TH	8.30 AM	H OR's taking position for Anti Tank Gun	AV3
ST JEAN	—		Remainder of Battery resting, H OR at Signal School	AV3
Sht.28 D13.F80	30TH	8.30 AM	H OR's taking position for Anti Tank Gun	AV3
BELLEVUE	—	6.30 AM	3 OR's unloading material for Gun position	AV3
ST JEAN	—		Remainder of Battery resting, Remainder T Battery	AV3
Sht.28 D13.F80	31st	8.30 AM	OR's taking position for Anti Tank Gun, H OR Guarding dummy gun position	AV3
ST JEAN	—		For Lieut. Battin Lieut. E.C. Bedford Rnn posted to X29 T.M.B. from Base	AV3
BELLEVUE	—	—	2 Officers + 20 OR's relieved Y Battery at Gun position	AV3
ST JEAN	—		Remainder of Battery resting, H OR at Signal School	AV3

W Barker
Capt. RFA
OC X/29 T.M.B.

Confidential.

War Diary

of

Y/29. T.M.B. R.A.

from
March 1st 1918. to March 31st 1918.

Volume 20.

Army Form C. 2118.

Y 29 T.M. Battery
(March 1918).

WAR DIARY
or
INTELLIGENCE SUMMARY.
(Erase heading not required.)

Place	Date	Hour	Summary of Events and Information	Remarks and references to Appendices
POPERINGHE	1st		1 Officer & 20 ORs Buck Fatigues YPRES. Remainder of Battery resting.	AM
" "	2nd 3rd 6th 7th	Noon	Gas Drill with Gas Helmets	AM
" "			1 Officer & 20 ORs Buck Fatigues YPRES. Remainder of Battery resting	AM
" "	4th		1 Officer & 16 ORs proceeded to St JEAN	PM
" "	5th		Remainder of Battery proceeded to VLAMERTINGHE and look over 8 M Division T.M. billets.	
St JEAN	6th		1 Officer & 16 ORs proceeded to BELLEVUE and took over gun positions from 8 M Division Trench Mortars	AM
VLAMERTINGHE	9th		8 ORs proceeded to St JEAN. Remainder of Battery at VLAMERTINGHE	AM
St JEAN	10th		8 ORs proceeded to forward positions to take over for 23 Troops batteries	AM
VLAMERTINGHE	11th		Remainder of Battery proceeded to St JEAN	AM
St JEAN	12th	7am	2 Officers & 10 ORs proceeded to BELLEVUE to relieve parties at BELLEVUE	AM
BELLEVUE	12th	7am	1 Officer & 10 ORs proceeded to VALOUR FARM. Zero on enemy's Trenches	AM
St JEAN	13th	7am	Ration party to BELLEVUE & OPs relieved. G.S. wagon from Brigade Dump to BELLEVUE to unload material	AM
BELLEVUE	14th	7am	Carrying material to VALOUR FARM. Fire on enemy's harbour area	AM

WAR DIARY
or
INTELLIGENCE SUMMARY.

Army Form C. 2118.

Y/29 T.M.B? March (Continued)

Place	Date	Hour	Summary of Events and Information	Remarks and references to Appendices
St Jean	15th	7th	4 OR's at Oxford Dump loading bombs and proceeded to Bellevue	NM
Vapour Farm	15th	7th	Firing on Enemy's Machine Gun & Trench Mortar emplacement	NM
— " —	16th	7th	Battery relieved by X/29 T.M.B?	NM
Bellevue	16th	7th	30 OR's carrying bombs etc to forward positions	NM
— " —	17th	7th	9 OR's carrying bombs to forward positions	NM
St Jean	18th	7th	3 OR's at Bilge Dump loading material & proceeding to Bellevue	NM
— " —	18th	7th	Camp under heavy shell fire from 8am to 6pm in Kurd Lane & Irish [?]	NM
Bellevue	19th	7th	22 OR's carrying bombs & material to Vapour Farm & Passchendaele	NM
St Jean	19th	7th	3 Officers OR's proceeded to Bellevue to relieve X/29 T.M.B.	NM
Bellevue	20th	7th	11 OR's carrying material to Vapour Farm	NM
St Jean	20th	7th	20 OR's wounded	NM
Vapour Farm	21st	8th	Firing on Enemy's Machine Gun emplacement	NM
Bellevue	22nd	7th	Carrying bombs to Vapour Farm	NM
Passchendaele	23rd	3rd	12 OR's making new positions	NM
Bellevue	24th	7th	Relieved by X/29 T.M.B?	NM
	25th	7th	4 OR's Reserve positions at R.F.A. 38	NM

WAR DIARY
or
INTELLIGENCE SUMMARY.

Army Form C. 2118.

J/29 T.M Bty
Ypres (Continued)

Place	Date	Hour	Summary of Events and Information	Remarks and references to Appendices
PASSCHENDAELE	26"	7th	1st ORs making new gun positions.	NM
St JEAN. Sheet 26 D.13. A.80	27"	7th	3 ORs at Oxford Dump loading bombs & proceeded to BELLEVUE.	NM
"	27"	7th	3 ORs making bunk beds & gun position.	NM
St JEAN	28"	7th	3 Officers & 15 ORs proceeded to BELLEVUE to relieve X/29 T.M. Bty.	NM
"	28"	7th	1 BR killed & 2 ORs wounded admitted to Hospital.	NM
"	28"	7th	3 ORs proceeded to BELLEVUE to replace casualties.	NM
"	29"	7th	6 ORs proceeded to new gun positions at PASSCHENDAELE	NM
"	29"	7th	4 ORs guarding Reserve gun positions at R.E.A. 38.	NM
PASSCHENDAELE	30"	7th	Heavy shelling on S.O.S. line.	NM
BELLEVUE	30"	7th	Carrying bombs to Vapour Farm. Fired on Enemy's T.M. emplacement from Vapour Farm.	NM
"	31"	7th	Carrying material to Vapour Farm	NM
"	31"	7th	Battery relieved by X/29 T.M. Bty.	NM

V. Sargent 2/Lt
O/C J/29 T.M Bty

29th Divisional Artillery.

X/29 TRENCH MORTAR BATTERY

APRIL 1918.

Confidential

War Diary

of

X/29 Trench Mortar Battery. R.A.

From: April 1st 1918 To April 30th 1918

Volume 21.

WAR DIARY
INTELLIGENCE SUMMARY.
(Erase heading not required.)

X 29 T.M.B.
(APRIL 1918)

Army Form C. 2118.

Place	Date	Hour	Summary of Events and Information	Remarks and references to Appendices
BELLEVUE	1st		Battery in action 4 O.R's at Signal School	A/3
ST JEAN	2nd			
"	3rd		Battery in action. 3 O.R's building Anti Tank position. 3 O.R's. reinforcing posts. 4 O.R's. Signal School	A/3
"	4th			
BELLEVUE	5th		Battery relieved by X Bty. 4 O.R's Signal School	A/3
ST JEAN	6th		Battery resting. 3 O.R's. fatigues on Anti Tank Gun position	B/3
"	7th		4 O.R. Signal School. Gas Helmet inspection	A/3
"	8th		Battery resting: 4 O.R's. Guarding Anti Gun position. 3 O.R's. Anti Tank position	A/3
"	9th		4 O.R. Signal School. Battery paid.	B/3
BELLEVUE	10th		Battery relieves Y. Bty. Gun position. 4 O.R. Signal School	B/3
"	11th		Battery in Action. reinforcing Gun position at VALOUR FARM	B/3
"	12th		Battery evacuates Gun position at VALOUR FARM and PASSCHENDAELE	B/3
"	-		Officers and Commander Reid. 16 O.R's. salvaged Guns & Ammunition	B/3
"	-		Battery moved to VLAMERTINGHE (ROAD CAMP)	B/3
VLAMERTINGHE	13th		Inspection by Lt. Col. D.A.C.	B/3
	14th	9-30	Inspection parade and smoke drill. 2.5. O.R. Ammunition fatigue at ST JEAN	B/3

WAR DIARY or INTELLIGENCE SUMMARY

Army Form C. 2118.

X 29 T.M.B.
(APRIL 1918)

Place	Date	Hour	Summary of Events and Information	Remarks and references to Appendices
VLAMERTINGHE	16TH	9.30 AM	Inspection Parade. 2 Officers & 21 O.Rs fatigues St JEAN. 1 O.R. Signal School	SV3
-.-	16TH	-.-	11 O.Rs fatigues for D.A. (Head Quarters)	SV3
-.-	17TH	-.-	2 Officers 50 O.Rs fatigues. Camp heavily shelled. Battery moved to	SV3
-.-			MARSH FARM.	SV3
-.-	18TH	9.30	Inspection Parade. 15 O.Rs fatigues various. V.Battery resting. 1 O.R. Signal School	SV3
-.-	19TH	2.0 AM	Inspection of equipment. 10 O.Rs fatigues. 1 O.R. Signal School.	SV3
-.-	20TH		Battery Resting	SV3
-.-	21st		2.8 O.Rs fatigues (Ammunition) 1 O.R. Signal School	SV3
-.-	22nd		Battery Paid	SV3
-.-	23rd	9.30	Inspection Parade. Physical Drill & Gas Helmet inspection. 1 O.R. Signal School	SV3
-.-	24TH			
-.-	25TH		Battery proceeded to POTIJZE * made Gun Positions. Battery delivered consecutively	SV3
-.-	26TH		Battery moved to HAMHOEK	SV3
HAMHOEK	27TH	10.0	Inspection Parade.	SV6
-.-	28TH		30 O.Rs fatigues sleeping at RED FARM	SV6 L
-.-	29TH		Battery disbanded temporarily. 2 Officers 7 O.Rs attached to 13TH Bde R.H.A. 1 Officer & 17TH Bde R.F.A. Remainder of Personnel to 29TH D.A.C.	SV30 LMC 30 OC XP 7 TMB

29th Divisional Artillery.

Y/29 TRENCH MORTAR BATTERY

APRIL 1918.

Confidential

— War Diary —

of

Y/29 Trench Mortar Battery. R.A.

From: April 1st 1918 To: April 30th 1918

Volume 21.

WAR DIARY
or
INTELLIGENCE SUMMARY.
(Erase heading not required.)

Army Form C. 2118.

of Y.29 T.M. Battery (April 1917)

Place	Date	Hour	Summary of Events and Information	Remarks and references to Appendices
ST JEAN	1st		Battery resting. 4 ORs Guarding Reserve Positions R.F.A. 38.	N.B.B
- " -	2nd		3 ORs Fatigues at Anti Tank Gun Position. Bathing Parade.	N.B.B
BELLEVUE	2nd		3 ORs Unloading bombs and material.	N.B.B
ST JEAN	3rd		1 NCO Guarding carrying party from BELLEVUE to 2nd positions	N.B.B
- " -	4th		4 ORs Anti Tank Gun Positions. 4 ORs relieved of Guard by X/29 T.M.B.	N.B.B
- " -	5th		1 OR Anti Tank Gun Position	N.B.B
BELLEVUE	5th		3 Officers & 20 ORs relieved X/29 T.M.B. Carrying bombs to Inspection	N.B.B
VAKOURFARM	6th		Fired 5 rounds in retaliation to Enemy's Trench Mortars	N.B.B
ST JEAN	6th		4 ORs Guarding Reserve Positions R.F.A. 38. 1 OR Anti Tank Gun Position	N.B.B
- " -	7th		3 ORs Anti Tank Gun Position	N.B.B
PASSCHENDAELE	7th		Registered on Enemy's T.M. Position	N.B.B
ST JEAN	8th		3 ORs loading material at SPREE FARM and proceeded to BELLEVUE	N.B.B
- " -	8th		4 ORs relieved of Guard by X/29 T.M.B.	N.B.B
- " -	9th		1 OR Unloading rations at BELLEVUE	N.B.B
BELLEVUE	10th		4 ORs Orderlies	N.B.B
ST JEAN	10th		4 ORs Guarding Reserve Positions. Battery relieved from positions by X/29 T.M.B.	N.B.B. J.L.M.

WAR DIARY
or
INTELLIGENCE SUMMARY. April (Contd)

Army Form C. 2118.

(Erase heading not required.)

Place	Date	Hour	Summary of Events and Information	Remarks and references to Appendices
BELLEVUE	11th	7h	1. OR Orderly	24ws
ST JEAN	12th	7h	Hors relieved off guard by x/29 T.M.B4. Battery left ST JEAN and	24ws
			proceeded to ROAD CAMP	24ws
ROAD CAMP	13th	9 a.m.	Colonel's Inspection	24ws
ST JEAN	14th	7h	1 Officer & 25 ORs Fatigues	24ws
"	15th	7h	1 Officer & 15 ORs Fatigues	24ws
DEAD END	15th	7pm	5 ORs Fatigues for D.A.	24ws
"	16th	7h	1 Officer & 10 ORs Fatigues for D.A.	24ws
ROAD CAMP	17th	7h	Camp heavily shelled. 1 Officer & 15 ORs WIELTJE Salvaging	24B.B
"	17th	7h	Battery removed to VLAMERTINGHE. 1 Officer & 15 ORs ST JEAN Fatigues	24B.B
VLAMERTINGHE	18th	7h	15 ORs ST JEAN Salvaging	24B.B
"	19th	7h	10 ORs — " —	24B.B
"	20th	7h	Battery resting	24B.B
"	21st		1 Officer & 27 ORs WIELTJE Salvaging	24B.B
WIELTJE	22nd	2pm	Digging French Mortar positions	24B.B
"	23rd	2pm	Digging French Mortar positions	24ws

WAR DIARY
or
INTELLIGENCE SUMMARY

Army Form C. 2118.

April (cont'd).

Place	Date	Hour	Summary of Events and Information	Remarks and references to Appendices
VRAMERTINGHE	24th		6 ORs rejoined Y/29 Battery from 29th D.A.C. 11 ORs returned to 29th D.A.C.	WBB
"			6 ORs proceeded to WIEKTJE	
WIEKTJE	25th		6 ORs proceeded to WIEKTJE	WBB
VRAMERTINGHE	25th		Battery ordered to return to VRAMERTINGHE	WBB
"	26th		2 ORs posted to Battery from 29th D.A.C.	WBB
"			3 Officers & 38 ORs proceeded to HAMHOEK 14 ORs remained at 29th D.A as covering party.	WBB
HAMHOEK	27th		14 ORs returned from D.A.	WBB
"	28th		1 Officer & 43 remaining H.Q. field ambul.	WBB
"	29th		1 Officer & 9 ORs temporarily attached to 15th Bde R.H.A (2nd S.D.A.)	WBB
			to 17th Bde R.F.A.	
			2 Officers & 2 ORs Remainder of personnel and transport temporarily attached to 29th D.A.C.	Yes
HAMHOEK	30th	9.0 AM	Inspection by Officer Comdg No 2 Section, 29th D.A.C.	WBA
			W.B.B. DeLee Lieut. R.F.A.	
			0/c Y/29 T.M. B.14	

Confidential

War Diary

of

X/29th Trench Mortar Battery. R.A.

From May 1st 1918 To May 31st 1918

Volume 22.

WAR DIARY or INTELLIGENCE SUMMARY

Army Form C. 2118.

X/29 T.M. Battery (MAY 1915)

Place	Date	Hour	Summary of Events and Information	Remarks and references to Appendices
HMMOCK	1st		Battery attached to No.1 Section Bg TH DAC 2 officers & a detachment K.15th	A/3
—	12th		Bde RHA 10 Officers & NCOs left our T.M. position for 6th Div TMS	A/3
—			at YPRES	A/3
—	13th		Battery returned. 1 Officer & 1 O.R. aposted from 15th Bde RHA 1 officer NCOs at	A/3
—			Gun position YPRES	A/3
—	14th		Battery moved from HMMOCK to take over WALLON CAPPEL and Gun Rt. Pr	A/2
—	15th		at	A/2
WALLON CAPPEL	16th		No 3 Section 54th DAC 1 officer 11 ORs Gun position YPRES	A/3
—	17th		Fatigue for No3 Section. Made 6 new guns NE U.27 to 22 Von Wagon 58 ORs	A/3
—	18th		Resting Camp. 11 ORs 1 Officer returned from YPRES	A/3
—	18th		Fatigue on camp. 1 officer & 6 relieving in for 17th Bde RHA	A/3
SEC-BOIS	19th		2 Officers 58 ORs passed forward to motor transport Gun position YO15 supported	A/3
—			men from 15th Bde RHA	A/3
—	20th		10 ORs moved to forward position	A/3
SEC BOIS	21st		Battery forwards making good gun position at 6B1B to FLERRY	A/3
—	25th		Battery relieved by Y/29 and E25 B86	A/3

Army Form C. 2118.

WAR DIARY
INTELLIGENCE SUMMARY
(Erase heading not required.)

X/29 T.M. Battery
(MAY 1918)

Place	Date	Hour	Summary of Events and Information	Remarks and references to Appendices
WALLON CAPPEL	26th	8-30	BATTERY RESTING:- Inspection parade by O.C. Battery	
		9.10	Gun Drill with Gas Helmets	
		10.30 a.m	Marching Drill	
	27th	9 am	Inspection parade	
		"	Gun Drill and Physical Exercises	
	29th	2 PM	Inspection parade. Went over ground forward of Gun positions	
	30th	9-0 AM	Battery on Gun Drill	
		10 AM	Physical Exercises	
SEC BOIS	31st		Battery moved forward to Gun positions E27075 E16A97 and E25436 to relieve X/29	

J.M. Barker
Capt. X/29 T.M.B.
O.C. X/29 T.M.B.

Confidential

— War Diary —

of

Y/29 Trench Mortar Battery. R.A.

From May 1st 1918 To May 31st 1918

Volume 22.

WAR DIARY or INTELLIGENCE SUMMARY

Army Form C. 2118.

8 Y29 T.M Battery

(Erase heading not required.)

Place	Date	Hour	Summary of Events and Information	Remarks and references to Appendices
MANHOCK	1st		10.0am 9 O.R.s attached to 15th Bde R.H.A. 2 O.R.s attached to D.A.M.S.	843
"	10th/12th		" " " " " 1st M. Bde R.F.A.	243
"	"		Remainder of Personnel did visual work	243
"	12th		8 O.R.s took over Trench Mortar Sections from 6th T.M Bde	1/3
MANHOCK	13th		Reorganisation of 30th Trench Mortar	8/2
CARPEL	14th		18 O.R.s attached to 3rd Section 29th D.A.C.	2/2
"	15th		Entering Camp	
"	16th		8 O.R.s returned from YPRES	343
"	"		9.0am Marching drill 10.30am Gun drill 3.0pm Inspection Parade	
"	10th		1 Officer and O.R returned from 15th Bde R.F.A. 2 officers & 9 O.R.s returned from 1st Bde	
"	20th/21st		9.0am Marching drill 10.30am Gun drill 3.0pm Inspection Parade	
"	22nd		10.0am Visitors Preceded by forward camp Sec Bois	
"	"		Taking Trench Mortar Position	
L.O.D	23rd			
WAHLON CAPPEN	24th		26 O.R.s Preceded to forward camp Sec Bois	
L.N.A.O	25th		Taking Trench Mortar Position	

Army Form C. 2118.

WAR DIARY
or
INTELLIGENCE SUMMARY.
(Erase heading not required.)

...... 4th (Howr.) ....

Instructions regarding War Diaries and Intelligence Summaries are contained in F.S. Regs., Part II. and the Staff Manual respectively. Title pages will be prepared in manuscript.

Place	Date	Hour	Summary of Events and Information	Remarks and references to Appendices
Sec. Bois	Oct 16		Carrying material to position at F.16.A.9 and E.35.B.86	8/3
	17		Carrying material to position at E.21.D.95	8/3
	18		Making positions	8/3
	19		Cutting gun pits at position E.21.D.95 and F.16.A.9	8/3
	20		Cutting gun pits at position E.35.B.86	8/3
	29		Fired in cooperation to Execute French Horace	8/3
Ind A 4c 30		Battery moved up + 27 I.M.Blk	8/3
	31			

M.W. Jay
Capt. R.F.A.
4/30 I.M.Stky

Confidential

War Diary

of

Y/29th Trench Mortar Battery R.A.

From June 1st 1918 To June 30th 1918

Volume 23

WAR DIARY
INTELLIGENCE SUMMARY

Army Form C. 2118.

X/29 T.M. Battery
June 1918

Place	Date	Hour	Summary of Events and Information	Remarks and references to Appendices
Sec Bois	1		Battery resting.	
-"-	2nd			
-"-	3rd		Carrying ammunition and material to positions.	
Sh.62.F.13.b N.E.	4th		Relieved X 29 T.M. Bty.	
-"-	5th		Digging positions at E.16.A and D.	
-"-	6th		Carrying material to positions at E.27.D, E.22.B, E.16.A and A.	
-"-	7th		30 rounds on enemy target.	
-"-	8th		Relieved by X/29 T.M. Bty.	
Sec Bois	9th		Resting.	
-"-	10th			
-"-	11th			
-"-	12th		Battery relieved X 29 T.M. Bty.	
Sh.62.F.13.b N.E.	13th		2 O.Rs at E.22.B. Remainder of battery at Sec Bois.	
-"-	14th		6 O.Rs at E.22.B.	
-"-	15th		1 O.R killed 1 O.R wounded. No.203 Gunner Dunn blown up of emplacement at E.22.B.	
-"-	16		Relieved by X/29 T.M. Bty.	
Sec Bois	17		9 a.m. Marching out. 2.30 p.m. Marching into Cor: Grassid	
-"-	to 20th		1 O.R Gassed. Camp heavily shelled, removed to D.15.d.35.70.	

WAR DIARY
INTELLIGENCE SUMMARY.
(Erase heading not required.)

Army Form C. 2118.

Instructions regarding War Diaries and Intelligence Summaries are contained in F. S. Regs., Part II. and the Staff Manual respectively. Title pages will be prepared in manuscript.

Place	Date	Hour	Summary of Events and Information	Remarks and references to Appendices
SHEET 36 NE A1	21		Relieved X/29 T.M.Bty.	
	22		22 rounds fired on selected targets.	
-"-	23		20 rounds -"-	
-"-	24		Relieved by X/29 T.M.Bty.	
D15 A35 70	25	9.0 A.M.	Saluting Drill. 2.0 P.M. Marching Drill.	
-"-	26	9.0 A.M.	Marching Drill. 2.0 P.M. Gas Attack Drill.	
-"-	27			
SHEET 13 NE A9	28		Relieved X/29 T.M.Bty. 110 rounds fired creeping barrage in support of attack	
-"-	29			
-"-	30		Repairing positions.	

J. Barnes
Capt. R.F.A.
of Y/29 T.M.Bty.

Confidential

War Diary

of

X/29th Trench Mortar Battery. R.A.

From June 1st 1918 To June 30th 1918

Volume 23

WAR DIARY
or
INTELLIGENCE SUMMARY.
(Erase heading not required.)

X/29 T.M. Battery. June 1918

Army Form C. 2118.

Place	Date	Hour	Summary of Events and Information	Remarks and references to Appendices
SHEET 36A N.E.	1st		Battery in action 3 Emplacements at E.27.D	843
			— // — E.22.B	
			— // — E.16.A and D	
			Selected targets. Fired 10 rounds on SOS	843
— // —	2nd		Carrying ammunition to positions	843
— // —	3rd		Creeping barrage in support of attack on ANKLE and PUG FARMS	843
			110 rounds fired. 1 O.R. Wounded.	843
			Relieved by J/29 T.M.By.	843
SEC BOIS	4th			843
	5th		Resting	843
	6th			
	7th		1 O.R. wounded.	
	8th		Carrying ammunition to positions	843
SHEET 36A N.E.	9th		Relieved J/29 T.M.By. 1 O.R. wounded	843
			10 rounds fired on selected targets	
— // —	10th		20 rounds fired on — // —	843
— // —	11th		30 rounds fired on — // —	843
— // —	12th		Relieved by Y/29 T.M.By.	843
SEC BOIS	13th		Resting	843
	14th		Carrying ammunition to positions	843
— // —	15th		Resting	843
SHEET 36A N.E.	16th		Carrying material to positions. Relieved Y/29 T.M.By.	843

WAR DIARY of INTELLIGENCE SUMMARY.

X/29 T.M. Battery (June 1918 Cont'd)

Army Form C. 2118.

Place	Date	Hour	Summary of Events and Information	Remarks and references to Appendices
SHEET 3/A	17TH		30 rounds fired at selected targets.	843
-"-	18TH		Repairing positions	843
-"-	19TH/20TH		Carrying ammunition and material to positions. Replaced No.2 gun at F22B.	843
-"-	21ST		Relieved by Y/29 T.M.Bty.	843
D16A3570	22ND		Resting	
-"-	23RD		9.0 am Marching drill	#3
-"-	24TH		9.0 am Marching drill	843
SHEET 3/6 W.E.	25TH		Relieved Y/29 T.M. Bty.	843
-"-	26TH		Carrying ammunition to positions.	843
-"-	27TH		30 rounds fired on selected targets	843
-"-	28TH		Carrying ammunition to positions	843
D15A3540	29TH		Relieved by Y/29 T.M.Bty.	843
-"-	30TH		9.0 am Marching drill 2pm Inspection 2.0 pm	843
			9.0 am Ditto -"-	

W Bosley
Capt. R.F.A.
O/C X/29 T.M. Battery

Confidential

War Diary

of

X/29th Trench Mortar Battery. R.A.

From July 1st 1918: To July 31st 1918

Volume 24

WAR DIARY or INTELLIGENCE SUMMARY

Army Form C. 2118.

X/29. T.M. Battery
(July 1918)

(Erase heading not required.)

Place	Date	Hour	Summary of Events and Information	Remarks and references to Appendices
Sheet 28 NE DISHYO	1st		Battery Resting	Nil.
"	2nd		9AM Marching Drill & Saluting Drill. 2PM Gas Helmet Inspection & Drill	Nil.
BANDRINGHEM	3rd		Relieved by 31st DIV T.M. Moved by lorries to Camp near BANDRINGHEM	Nil.
"	4th		9AM Clearing up Camp etc. 2PM Swimming parade	Nil.
"	5th to 9th		9AM Inspection parade. Rifle & Gun Drill. 2PM Rifle & Gun Drill & Swimming	Nil. Nil.
"	9th		Divisional Horse Show. Battery paid 6th	Nil.
"	10th		8AM Baths. 11-30 Inspection parade. 2-30 PM Inspection by Army Commander.	Nil.
"	11th to 12th		9AM Inspection & Games. 11AM Gun Drill. 2PM Rifle practice	Nil.
"	21st		Battery paid 20th	Nil.
"	22nd		Removed to COIN PERDU (marched) erected camp	Nil.
COIN PERDU	23rd to 29th		9AM Inspection parade. 11AM Gun & Rifle Drill. 2PM Rifle practice & Swimming 2PM Marching drill & Gas Helmet Drill. Battery paid 26th	Nil. Nil.

Army Form C. 2118.

WAR DIARY
or
INTELLIGENCE SUMMARY.
(Erase heading not required.)

69 x/30 TMB

Place	Date	Hour	Summary of Events and Information	Remarks and references to Appendices
COIMPE R DU	30th	9 AM	Inspection parade. 10 AM Gun Drill. 5 PM Games.	
—	31st	9 AM	Inspection parade. 10.30 Inspection by Divisional Commander	

Confidential

— War Diary —

of

Y/29 Trench Mortar Battery RA

From July 1st 1918 : To July 31st 1918.

Volume 24

WAR DIARY
of
INTELLIGENCE SUMMARY.
(Erase heading not required.)

"Y" 29 T.M Battery
July 1918.

Army Form C. 2118.

Place	Date	Hour	Summary of Events and Information	Remarks and references to Appendices
E17D SHEET 36A NE	1st		Battery in action	
-11-	3rd		Relieved by 31st D.T.M. Mortar Battery and went to join near BEAURAINGHEM	
BAURAINGHEM	4th		Gymnastic parade	
-11-	5th		9.0 AM Swimming Parade 2.0 PM Swimming Parade	
-11-	6th		9.0 AM Inspection Parade. Rifle & Gun drill. 2.0 Pm Gun drill & Swimming	
-11-	7th		Divisional Horse Show	
-11-	8th		8.0 AM Baths. 11.30 AM Inspection Parade 2.0 PM Inspection by Brig. Commander	
-11-	10th		9.0 AM Inspection Parade. Rifle & Gun drill 2.0 PM Rifle drill & Swimming	
-11-	11th-21st		Removed to COINPERDU (marched) erected Camp	
COINPERDU	22nd			
-11-	29th		9.0 AM Inspection Parade. Gun drill. Lewis gun, Rifle drill	
-11-	30th		9.0 AM Inspection Parade. 10.0 AM Gun drill S.O. Games	
-11-	31st		9.0 AM Inspection Parade 10.30 AM Inspection by Divisional Commander	

Capt. commdg. B.F.A
for Y29 T.M.Bty

Confidential

— War Diary —

of

X/29th Trench Mortar Battery RA

August 1st 1918   To   August 31st 1918

Volume 25

Army Form C. 2118.

WAR DIARY

INTELLIGENCE SUMMARY.

1/29 T.M.B.

(Erase heading not required.)

Place	Date	Hour	Summary of Events and Information	Remarks and references to Appendices
COIN PERDU	1st		Battery Resting	Sgt.
STRAZEELE	2nd		Relieved 1st Australian Trench Mortar Battery. 8 guns in support + 4 guns in action	Sgt.
"	"		Battery Headquarters at E 4 d. 50.40.	Sgt.
"	"		Guns in action at No 1 Gun E 12 a 15.80. No 2 Gun E 12 90.10.	Sgt.
"	"		No 3 " X 25 & 30.50. No 2 How Y 25 & 80.30.	Sgt.
"	"		Guns in support at No 7 " E 4 c 32.62 No 2 Gun E 4 C 40.90	Sgt.
"	"		No 3 " W 29 a 93.09 No 4 " W 29 & 02.09	Sgt.
"	"		No 5 " W 24 a 50.62 No 6 " W 24 a 55.70	Sgt.
"	"		No 4 " X 19 a 20.90 No 8 " X 19 a 30.90	Sgt.
"	"		Relief completed by 9.30 P.M.	Sgt.
"	3rd		Cleaned guns, repaired gun pits, carried ammunition	Sgt.
"	4th		Built dug out at W 34 C.S.S. Carried 30 rounds of ammunition to 2 gun. Cleaned gun	Sgt.
"	5th		Building dugout. Carried ammunition to no 1 - 2 gun. Cleaned guns	Sgt.
"	6th		Established communication both centre section firing batteries	Sgt.
"	"		Watered 1 to 2 gun. Cleaned guns	Sgt.
"	7th		Carried ammunition to No's 2 + 4 guns. Built ammunition	Sgt.
"	"		recesses at No's 2 + 4 gun positions	Sgt.

WAR DIARY
or
INTELLIGENCE SUMMARY.
(Erase heading not required.)

X/29 T.M.B.

Army Form C. 2118.

Place	Date	Hour	Summary of Events and Information	Remarks and references to Appendices
STRAZEELE	7th		Cleaned reserve guns	Sgt.
	8th		Carried ammunition to no. 1 and no. 2 guns by pack mule and by land. Improved gun position.	Sgt. Sgt.
	9th		Cleaned guns. Relieved by Y/29 T.M.B. at H.O. P.M. Marched to rest camp.	Sgt. Sgt.
HONDEGHEM	10th		9 A.M. Bath. 2 P.M. Physical Service	Sgt. Sgt. Sgt.
	11th		1 officer and 9 other ranks returned from II Army T.M. School. 9 A.M. Inspection parade & gundrill. 2 P.M. Physical Service & anti-gas drill.	Sgt.
	12th		6 A.M. Physical Service. 9 A.M. Inspection parade & kit inspection. 2 P.M. marching and saluting drill	Sgt. Sgt.
† 13	13th		5 other ranks to II Army trench mortar school. 6 A.M. Physical Service. 9 A.M. Inspection parade & gun drill. 2 P.M. Bathing & Box respirator drill. 2 other ranks to II Army rest camp. 2 other ranks to England for tour of duty at home.	Sgt. Sgt. Sgt. Sgt. Sgt.
	14th		6 A.M. Physical drill. 9 A.M. Inspection parade and marching drill. 2 P.M. Bathing and Box respirator drill. 1 officer posted to Battery.	Sgt. Sgt. Sgt. Sgt.
	15th		6 A.M. Physical drill. 9 A.M. Inspection parade and anti gas drill. 2 P.M. Bathing and marching drill.	Sgt. Sgt. Sgt.

Army Form C. 2118.

WAR DIARY
or
INTELLIGENCE SUMMARY.
(Erase heading not required.)

X/29. T.M.B.

Instructions regarding War Diaries and Intelligence Summaries are contained in F.S. Regs. Part II. and the Staff Manual respectively. Title pages will be prepared in manuscript.

Place	Date	Hour	Summary of Events and Information	Remarks and references to Appendices
STRAZEELE	16th		Relieved X/29 T.M.B. in the line. Relief completed by 6 A.M. Carried ammunition to Nos 1, 3, and 4 guns.	Sut
	17th		Registered guns for creeping operation of 9th and 29th Division on HOEGENACKER SPUR. Fired 12 rounds. Established telephonic communication with Infantry Battalions and Brigade. Carried ammunition. En route for dugout.	Sut Sut Sut
	18th		Nos 1, 3, & 4 guns fired in support of operation. Fired 1944 rounds. Built a dugout forward for centre section at X.25.a.40.60.	Sut
	19th		Built a telephone pit at STRAZEELE STATION. Carried ammunition.	Sut
	20th		Moved Nos 1 and 4 guns forward to support new line.	Sut Sut
	21st		Moved Nos 3 gun forward to approximate new position at F3C.25.75. Carried ammunition.	Sut Sut
	22nd		Carried ammunition forward to new position and dug pits.	Sut
	23rd		Cleaned guns. Relieved by Y/29 T.M.B. at 4 P.M. Marched to rest camp at HONDEGHEM.	Sut Sut
	24th		9 A.M. Baths. 2 P.M. Physical drill.	Sut

Army Form C. 2118.

WAR DIARY
or
INTELLIGENCE SUMMARY.
(Erase heading not required.)

of 8/ 1/29 T.M.B

Place	Date	Hour	Summary of Events and Information	Remarks and references to Appendices
HONDEGHEN.	25th		Battery resting and training {	Sub.
	26th	1 A.M.	Physical drill.	Sub.
	27th	9 A.M.	Inspection parade. Gundrill and Anti Gas drill.	Sub.
	28th	2 P.M.	Marching drill and bathing.	Sub.
	29th			Sub.
"	30th		1 Officer to 15th Brigade R.H.A. 1 Officer posted from 29th D.A.C.	Sub. Sub. Sub.
PRADELLES	31st		moved to harness. W/16c 14.07. (nr. PRADELLES) 1 Officer + 25 other ranks assisted 491 Coy R.E. to repair roads from E.4, S.9, + E.5.C.17. Remainder collecting guns etc.	Sub. Sub. Sub.

Salmon 2/Lt RFA
for O.C. X/29 T.M.B.

Confidential

— War Diary —

of

Y/29th Trench Mortar Battery. R.A

August 1st 1918   To August 31st 1918

Volume 25

WAR DIARY
INTELLIGENCE SUMMARY.
(Erase heading not required.)

Army Form C. 2118.

Y/29 Trench Mortar Battery

Place	Date	Hour	Summary of Events and Information	Remarks and references to Appendices
COINPERDU	1-8-18		Battery Resting	W/m
HONDEGHEM	2ND		Relieved 1st Australian Trench Mortar Battery	W/m
	3·8·18 to 9·8·18		Battery Training. Gun drill. Gas mask drill etc.	W/m
STRAZEELE	9th		Relieved X battery in the line	W/m
	10th		Carried ammunition and cleaned Guns	W/m
	11th		Reconnoitred ground around CELERY COTTAGES and decided to put Gun	W/m
			No 1 Gun (E.12.A.6.0) registered	W/m
	12th		No 1 Gun (E.12.A.6.0) registered	W/m
	13th		Bombs carried up to No 1 Gun during night 13th/14th in preparation for forthcoming attack.	W/m
	14th		Area around SCARP COTTAGES reconnoitred for Gun positions but found unsuitable.	W/m
			Guns at X.25.B.27.55 moved forward to X/.25.A.80.10	W/m
	15th		Bombs carried up to No 3 & 4 Guns at X.25.A.80.10 in preparation for coming attack.	W/m
	16th		No 3 and 4 Guns registered on Selected Targets 2·18 rounds fired. Relieved in the line by X Battery	W/m

Army Form C. 2118.

WAR DIARY
or
INTELLIGENCE SUMMARY.
(Erase heading not required.)

1/9 T M B

Instructions regarding War Diaries and Intelligence Summaries are contained in F. S. Regs., Part II. and the Staff Manual respectively. Title pages will be prepared in manuscript.

Place	Date	Hour	Summary of Events and Information	Remarks and references to Appendices
HONDEGHEM	17th to 22nd		Battery training. Physical Exercises. Gas drill with Gas masks etc	Appx
STRAZEELE	23rd		Relieved X Battery in the line, relief completed by 5.30.10 a.m.	Appx
	24th		Bombs carried and Guns cleaned. 20 rounds fired on the Trucks, E. of CELERY COPSE	Appx
	25th		Positions reconnoitred and located as at F.11.b.5.9. to engage DESPOT FARM. and DROOMARA.	Appx
	26th		Owing to reported change in Divisional Boundary, positions at F.11.b.5.9. abandoned. Orders to get in 4 Guns to support Y Lines Positions reconnoitred and F.3.C.33.70 (No 1) & F.3.C.35.73.24 (No 2) decided on, material carried to No 1 Gun.	Appx
	27th		Material & Bombs carried to No 1 & 2 Gun positions. All guns and material transferred from S. to N. of the Railway owing to the change in Divisional Boundary	Appx
	28th		No 1 gun position completed & Bombs carried up by Infantry carrying party. Positions at BELLE CROIX FARM. Reconnoitred & started on.	Appx

Army Form C. 2118.

WAR DIARY
or
INTELLIGENCE SUMMARY.
(Erase heading not required.)

of 7/29 TMB

Place	Date	Hour	Summary of Events and Information	Remarks and references to Appendices
STRAZEELE	29th		2 Pits dug at BELLE CROIX FARM. Ammunition carried up by Pack Mules to Nos 1 & 3 positions. No 1 Gun registered & 12 rounds fired on GANDER CROSSING No 2 Gun position completed.	Appx — Appx —
	30th		Mortar work discontinued and all Gunners to have one day's refreshing according to the army retirement.	Appx —
OUTTERSTEENE	31st		Repairing and re-adjusting the equipment until the 497 Field Coy R.E.	Appx —

(signed) A. Knudly Capt.
OC 7/29 TMB

Confidential

— War Diary —

of

X/29th Trench Mortar Battery. R.A.

From September 1st 1918: To September 30th 1918

Volume 26.

WAR DIARY
INTELLIGENCE SUMMARY.

X/R9 T.M.B. (SEPTEMBER.)

Army Form C. 2118.

Place	Date	Hour	Summary of Events and Information	Remarks and references to Appendices
STRAZEELE	1st		One Officer & 25 O.Rs repairing roads under supervision of R.E⁵ at VERITY CROSSING	2W3
"	"		F5 C.20.55 & FURLOUGH G CROSS. FU. C45.80. Brought out beds & cans from old positions	2W3
"	2nd		One Officer & 25 O.Rs R.E. fatigues at VERITY CROSSING. Brought out remainder of kits and guns from old positions. Taking T.M. Ammunition	4W3
"	3rd		One Officer & 25 O.Rs R.E. fatigues at VERITY CROSSING & Cleaning guns	2W3
"	4th		One Officer & 25 O.Rs R.E. fatigues at F.12.A.80.35, & Cleaning Guns	1W3
"	5th		Established a forward dump at LA CRECHE for one officer and 25 O.R¹⁵ in conjunction with R.E. fatigues. 10 O.Rs would work here for morning party	2W3
"	"		completion of days work	2W3
BAILLEUL and STEENWERK	7th		R.E. fatigues Repairing roads between BAILLEUL and STEENWERK.	3W3
"	8th			1W3
"	9th		R.E. fatigues. Repairing roads between BAILLEUL and STEENWERK. Battery H.Q. moved from STRAZEELE to LA CRECHE.	9W3
"	10th			2W3
"	11th		R.E. fatigues Repairing roads between BAILLEUL and STEENWERK.	3W3
BORRE	12th		Battery moved to BORRE. 27/ W. Gall.	2W3
"	13th		Taking T.M Ammunition	2W3
"	14th			4W3

WAR DIARY or INTELLIGENCE SUMMARY.

Army Form C. 2118.

X/49 T.M.B. (SEPTEMBER)

Place	Date	Hour	Summary of Events and Information	Remarks and references to Appendices
DROGLANDT	15th		Moved by motor lorries to DROGLANDT. K51A03.	
"	16th to 22nd		Gun drill, Rifle drill, Physical Exercise & Games. Gas Drill (all ranks wore gas masks for one hour daily whilst performing duties).	
VLAMERTINGHE	23rd		Moved to VLAMERTINGHE by Light Railway	
"	24th to 26th		Inspection Parades. Gun laying and Physical Exercise	
"	27th		24 O.R.s making forward dumps of T.M. ammn for 123 A.F. Brigade. Battery moved to YPRES	
YPRES	28th to 30th		2 Officers and 10 N.C.Os did reconnaissance on newly captured ground remainder of Battery following up the infantry repairing roads in conjunction with R.E.s. HQrs.	
			Proceed to II Army School for T.M. course	

Confidential

— War Diary —

of

Y/29 Trench Mortar Battery. R.A.

From September 1st 1918: To September 30th 1918

Volume 26.

Army Form C. 2118.

WAR DIARY
or
INTELLIGENCE SUMMARY.
(Erase heading not required.)

1/29 Trench Mortar Battery
September 1918

Instructions regarding War Diaries and Intelligence Summaries are contained in F. S. Regs., Part II. and the Staff Manual respectively. Title pages will be prepared in manuscript.

Place	Date	Hour	Summary of Events and Information	Remarks and references to Appendices
BAILLEUL and	Sept 1st to 11th		Battery on combat duties with 497th Field Co. R.E. exchanging noses, destroyed by enemy air raids.	nil
STEENWERCKE	12th		2Lt Salway T.M. Lewis & Ammunition	nil
STRAZEELE				nil
BORRE	13th		Move into billets at BORRE	nil
STRAZEELE	14th		Battery repairs saving T.M. Ammunitions	nil
DROGLANDT	15th		Moved by lorry to DROGLANDT.	nil
	16th to 23rd		Battery training. Guns drill with Gas & ashes, Gas drill etc. (All ranks performed duties wearing Gas masks for 1 hour daily)	gave nil
VLAMERTINGHE	24th		Move to VLAMERTINGHE. On relaxation for forthcoming attack.	nil
	25th		Resting. Guns cleaned and overhauled.	nil
	26		"	nil
YPRES	27		March into action at YPRES ready for forthcoming attack.	nil
	28 to 30		Battery personnel repairing roads (newly captured ground) and co-operating with R.E. 1 officer & 3 OR's proceeded on course (TM) at II Army School.	nil

V.W. Cottrell
2/Lt R.F.A.
for O.C. 1/29 T.M.B.

Confidential

War Diary

of

X/29. Trench Mortar Battery. R.A.

From October 1st 1918 to October 31st 1918.

Volume. 27.

Army Form C. 2118.

WAR DIARY
or
INTELLIGENCE SUMMARY. X/29 T.M.B.
(Erase heading not required.)

(OCTOBER) 1918.

Place	Date	Hour	Summary of Events and Information	Remarks and references to Appendices
GLENCORSE WOOD.	1st to 3rd		Moved from YPRES to GLENCORSE WOOD. All available officers and men on road repairing under supervision of R.E's.	ON3 ON3
	2nd		Moved from GLENCORSE WOOD to YPRES.	ON3
	4– 6		Getting enemy 5.9 Hows. into new positions	ON3
	7– 10		One officer + 14 O.R.s moved to K10.a.10.40 Sheet 28 to man enemy 5.9 Hows. Remainder of Battery loading ammunition. Putting 6 mortars into action at ZEDEGHEM STATION.	ON3 ON3 ON3
ZEDEGHEM	11– 12		Battery firing enemy guns. (Fired 100 rounds)	ON3
	13– 14		Moved from YPRES to DADIZEELE & mortars on british remainder. One officer + B.S.M. firing enemy guns.	ON3 ON3
	15– 16		Today enemy guns.	ON3
BARRAKEN	17		Moved to BARRAKEN. One Officer and 24 O.R.s attached 1st Brigade R.F.A. One Officer + 6 O.R.s attached 149 D.9" (H.Q.) 4 O.R.s attached 146 Employment Coy.	ON3 ON3 ON3
HEULE	19		H.Q. moved to HEULE with D.A.C. H.Q.	ON3

Army Form C. 2118.

WAR DIARY
of X/29 T.M.B.
INTELLIGENCE SUMMARY
(Erase heading not required.)

(OCTOBER 18)

Place	Date	Hour	Summary of Events and Information	Remarks and references to Appendices
STAEGHEM	21st		Moved to Staeghem. H.Q. attached D.A.C.H.Q.	QMS
ST. BARBE	21st to 29th		Moved to St. Barbe. 1 Officer & 5 O.Rs. forward to II/Army T.M. School for course of instructions	QMS QMS
Note	17th to 31st		During this period personnel of Battery were attached for duty as follows:- 1 Officer 34 O.Rs 17th Bde R.F.A. 164. 6 O.Rs 29th D.A.C. 2 O.Rs att. 226 Employment Coy. & 8 O.Rs. were attending course of instruction at II Army T.M. School	QMS

A Barker
Capt R.F.A.
O.C. X/25 T.M.B.

Confidential

War Diary

of

Y/29 Trench Mortar Battery. R. A.

From October 1st 1918 to October 31st 1918.

Volume 27.

Army Form C. 2118.

WAR DIARY
of
INTELLIGENCE SUMMARY.
(Erase heading not required.)

1/2<u>9</u> Trench Mortar Battery

OCTOBER 1918

Instructions regarding War Diaries and Intelligence Summaries are contained in F. S. Regs., Part II. and the Staff Manual respectively. Title pages will be prepared in manuscript.

Place	Date	Hour	Summary of Events and Information	Remarks and references to Appendices
GLENCORSE WOOD	1st to 3rd		Battery moved to Glencorse Wood.	
	3rd		Reconning roads in conjunction with R.E.s	
	14th to 16th		Moved from Glencorse Wood to Ypres	
	17th to 10th		Getting away 5.9 Yser also pontoon to Ferro guns enemy	
			Battery machine gunning enemy 5.9 How at R10.a.10.40 (Sheet 28) also moving ammunition	
LEDEGHEM	11th to 12th		Putting 4 T.Ms into action at LEDEGHEM.	
			also firing many 5.9 Yser	
	13th to 16th		Moved from YPRES to DADIZEELE.	
			4 mortars in action also working many guns	
BARRAKEN	17th		Moved to BARRAKEN 2 off. 24 O.Rs attached on leave to 15th Brigade R.H.A.	
			8 O.Rs attached to 59th D.A.C. 4 O.Rs at 117th Brigade R.F.A.	
HEULE	19th		H.Q. moved to HEULE with H.Q. D.A.C.	
STAEGHEM	21st		Moved to STAEGHEM.	
St BARBE	27th		Moved to St BARBE	

Army Form C. 2118.

WAR DIARY
or
INTELLIGENCE SUMMARY.
(Erase heading not required.)

No. 29 T.M.B. (Cavoli)

OCTOBER 1918

Instructions regarding War Diaries and Intelligence Summaries are contained in F. S. Regs., Part II. and the Staff Manual respectively. Title pages will be prepared in manuscript.

Place	Date	Hour	Summary of Events and Information	Remarks and references to Appendices
	17th to 31st		During this position personnel of this Battery were attached for duty as follows. 2 Off. 24 O.Rs. 15th "B" Bugd. R.H.A. 8 O.Rs. 29th D.A.C. 4 O.Rs. 17th Bde R.F.A.	
			1 Off. 4 O.Rs. attending course of instruction at II Army T.M. School.	
	29th		5 O.Rs. to II Army T.M. School for demonstration duties of T.M. work.	

Morton Capt. R.A.
for O.C. Y/29 TMB.

C O F I D E N T I A L.

WAR DIARY.

OF

X/29 TRENCH MORTAR BATTERY R.A.

1st November 1918 to 30th November 1918.

Volume 28.

Army Form C. 2118.

WAR DIARY
of
INTELLIGENCE SUMMARY.
(Erase heading not required.)

X/29 T.M.B.   NOVEMBER.

Instructions regarding War Diaries and Intelligence Summaries are contained in F. S. Regs. Part II. and the Staff Manual respectively. Title pages will be prepared in manuscript.

Place	Date	Hour	Summary of Events and Information	Remarks and references to Appendices
RONCQ.	1st.		Battery reformed. Equipped with mobile mortars.	W3
TOURCOING.	3rd.		Moved to TOURCOING.	W3
TOINGUE.	8th.		Moved to TOINGUE.	W3
ST. GENOIS.	10th.		Moved to St. GENOIS.	W3
SEXXS.	13th.		Moved to SEXXS.	W3
WOBECQ.	15th.		Moved to WOBECQ.	W3
MARCQ.	18th.		Started March to German Frontier. Moved to MARCQ.	W3
SAINTES WISBECQ.	21st.		Moved to SAINTES WISBECQ.	W3
BRAINE ZAXXEUD	23rd.		Moved to BRAINE ZAXXEUD	W3
CHASTRE.	25th.		Moved to CHASTRE.	W3
GRAND - XEEZ.	27th.		Moved to GRAND XEEZ.	W3
WARET - XEVEQUE.	28th.		Moved to WARET LEVEQUE.	W3
STREE.	29th.		Moved to STREE.	W3
GEROMONT.	30th.		Moved to GEROMONT.	W3

Wright Capt. RFA.
ITMO 29 B.D.A.

COFIDENTIAL.

WAR DIARY.

OF

Y/29 TRENCH MORTAR BATTERY R.A.

1st November 1918 to 30th November 1918.

Volume 28.

WAR DIARY
or
INTELLIGENCE SUMMARY. 1/29 Trench Mortar Battery
NOVEMBER 1918
(Erase heading not required.)

Army Form C. 2118.

Place	Date	Hour	Summary of Events and Information	Remarks and references to Appendices
RONCQ	1-11-18		Battery resting	17pm
	2-11-18		" "	17pm
TURCOING	3-11-18		Move to TURCOING	17pm
				17pm
			Battery resting	
DOTTINGHE	4	8 am	March to DOTTINGHE	17pm
			Resting	17pm
				17pm
ST GENOSIS		9 am	Move to ST. GENOSIS	17pm
ARC ANNIÈRES		10 am	" ARC. ANNIÈRES	17pm
		11 am	Resting (limited Signal Hostilities ceasing at 11 am)	17pm
		12		17pm
WODECQ		13"	March commenced towards BANELAND. Battery moved to WODECQ.	17pm
			Resting	17pm
				17pm
BEVER		16	" to " BEVER	17pm
			Resting	17pm
		20		17pm
STEENKUP		21	March to STEENKUP	17pm
			Resting	17pm

Army Form C. 2118.

WAR DIARY
of
INTELLIGENCE SUMMARY

X/29 Trench Mortar Battery
NOVEMBER 1918

(Erase heading not required.)

Place	Date	Hour	Summary of Events and Information	Remarks and references to Appendices
MONT. ST. PONT.	23/11/18		March continued to MONT. ST. PONT.	App.
"	24th		Resting	App.
HEVILLERS	25th		March to HEVILLERS.	App.
"	26th		Resting	App.
SAUVENIR	27th		March continued to SAUVENIR	App.
FORVILLE	28th		" " — FORVILLE	App.
SARTE	29th		" " — SARTE	App.
GEROMONT	30th		" " — GEROMONT.	App.

Arnold Foster
Captain
O.C. X/29 T.M.B

No 29

War Diary

X/29 Trench Mortar Battery

DECEMBER 1918

T.M.O.
29th DIVISIONAL
ARTILLERY.

Army Form C. 2118.

WAR DIARY
or
INTELLIGENCE SUMMARY.   X/29 T.M.B

(Erase heading not required.)   (DECEMBER)

Instructions regarding War Diaries and Intelligence
Summaries are contained in F.S. Regs., Part II.
and the Staff Manual respectively. Title pages
will be prepared in manuscript.

Place	Date	Hour	Summary of Events and Information	Remarks and references to Appendices
GEROMONT	1st		Battery Resting.	A/3
	3rd		March Continued. Battery moved to RENOUCHAMPS.	A/3
RENOUCHAMPS	4th		Marched to FRANCORCHAMPS.	A/3
FRANCORCHAMPS	5th		Crossed the Frontier. Battery marched to WIESMES.	A/3
WIESMES	6th		Marched to MONTJOIE	A/3
MONTJOIE	7th		" " SCHMIDT.	A/3
SCHMIDT	8th		" " NIDDERSHEIM.	A/3
NIDDERSHEIM	9th		" " GLENIX.	A/3
GLENIX	10th		Battery Resting	A/3
	12th			
	13th		Marched to BERGGLADBACH (passing through COLOGNE, and across the RHINE)	A/3
BERGGLADBACH	13th to 31st		Battery forming part of Army of Occupation.	A/3

J Barber
Capt R.F.A.
2 i/c X/29 T.M.B

Army Form C. 2118.

WAR DIARY
or
INTELLIGENCE SUMMARY.   X/129 T.M.B.
(Erase heading not required.)   (DECEMBER)

Instructions regarding War Diaries and Intelligence Summaries are contained in F. S. Regs., Part II. and the Staff Manual respectively. Title pages will be prepared in manuscript.

Place	Date	Hour	Summary of Events and Information	Remarks and references to Appendices
GEROMONT	1st 2nd 3rd		Battery Resting.	
ENOUCHAMPS	4th		March Continued. Battery moved to RENOUCHAMPS.	
FRANCORCHAMPS	5th		Marched to FRANCORCHAMPS	
WIESMES	6th		Crossed the Frontier. Battery marched to WIESMES.	
MONTJOIE	7th		Marched to MONTJOIE	
SCHMIDT	8th		" " SCHMIDT.	
NUDDERSHEIM	9th		" " NUDDERSHEIM.	
GLENIZ	10th to 12th		" " GLENIZ. Battery Resting	
BERGGLADBACH	13th to 31st		Marched to BERGGLADBACH (passing through COLOGNE, and across the RHINE. Battery forming part of Army of Occupation.	

N Bradley
Capt RFA
O.C. X/129 T.M.B.

No 29.

War Diary
Y/29 Trench Mortar Battery

DECEMBER

T.M.O.
29th DIVISIONAL
ARTILLERY.
No.
Date.

WAR DIARY
INTELLIGENCE SUMMARY

1/89 T.M. Battery
DECEMBER 1918

Army Form C. 2118.

Place	Date	Hour	Summary of Events and Information	Remarks and references to Appendices
GEROMONT.	1st to 3rd		Battery Resting	JRH
AYWAILLE.	4th		March continued towards RHINELAND. Battery move to AYWAILLE.	JRH
NAVEZE.	5th		March to NAVEZE	JRH
MALMEDY.	6th		After overnight Battery crosses the frontier & marches to MALMEDY.	JRH
MONTJOIE	7th		— to MONTJOIE	JRH
ROLLESBROICH	8th		— ROLLES BROICH.	JRH
ZULPICH	9th		— ZULPICH	JRH
HURTH	10th, 11th & 12th		— HURTH	JRH
			Battery Resting	JRH
NAUENHAUS	13th		Battery to COLOGNE, crosses the RHINE to NAUENHAUS (Platz)	JRH
	14th to 20th		Battery Resting	JRH
BERG. GLADBACH	21st		Move to BERG. GLADBACH	2nd Lt
	22nd to 31st		Battery becoming part of Army of Occupation	JRH

J.R. Moore 2nd Lt RGA
1/20 1 MTB

Army Form C. 2118.

WAR DIARY

~~INTELLIGENCE SUMMARY~~ X/səg T. M. Battery

(Erase heading not required.)

DECEMBER 1918

Instructions regarding War Diaries and Intelligence Summaries are contained in F.S. Regs. Part II. and the Staff Manual respectively. Title pages will be prepared in manuscript.

Place	Date	Hour	Summary of Events and Information	Remarks and references to Appendices
BEAUMONT	1st to 3rd		Battery Resting.	
AYWAILLE	4th		March continued towards RHINELAND. Battery move to AYWAILLE.	
MYNEZEE	5th		March to MYNEZEE	
MALMEDY	6th		At first halt place. Battery cross the frontier & march to MALMEDY.	
MONTJOIE	7th		" " to MONTJOIE	
ROLLESBROICH	8th		" " — ROLLESBROICH	
ZULPICH	9th		" " — ZULPICH	
HURTH	10th 11th 12th		" " HURTH Battery Resting.	
NAUENHAUS	13th 14th		March through COLOGNE, crossed the RHINE to NAUEN HAUS (PLATZ) Battery Resting	
	20th		" to BERG. GLADBACH	
BERG. GLADBACH	22nd to 31st		Battery forming 20 Pof Army of Occupation	

G.H.Ward 3/H RFA
Hon 3/H/B

RHINE ARMY
SOUTHERN DIVISION
LATE 29TH DIVISION

'X' & 'Y' TRENCH MORTAR BTTS.
JAN 1919

War Diary (X/29 T.M.B)
January 1919

Army Form C. 2118.

WAR DIARY
or
INTELLIGENCE SUMMARY. X/29 T.M.B
(Erase heading not required.)   (JANUARY)

Instructions regarding War Diaries and Intelligence Summaries are contained in F. S. Regs. Part II. and the Staff Manual respectively. Title pages will be prepared in manuscript.

Place	Date	Hour	Summary of Events and Information	Remarks and references to Appendices
BERGGLADBACH	1st to 5th		Field training carried out.	
"	6th to 9th		Battery sword cutting	
"	10th to 11th		Physical training	
	12th		1/2 O.R's attached to 15 Brigade R.H.A. for temporary duty	
	13th to 31st		Physical training, gun park fatigues etc 2 O.R's attached to 29th D.A.(H.Q) for temporary duty	

W Barker.
Capt R.F.a
Comg X/29 T.M.B.

Army Form C. 2118.

WAR DIARY
or
INTELLIGENCE SUMMARY. X/29 T.M.B
(Erase heading not required.) (JANUARY)

Place	Date	Hour	Summary of Events and Information	Remarks and references to Appendices
BERG GLADBACH	1st 2 to 5th		Field training carried out.	
	6th to 8th		Battery wood cutting	
	9th		Physical training	
	10th 11th		1 O.P.S. attached to 15" Brigade R.H.A. for temporary duty	
	12			
	13 to 31st		Physical training, gun park fatigues etc 2 O.P's attached to 29th D.A. (H.Q) for temporary duty.	

No 30

War Diary (Y/29 T.M.B).
January 1919.

WAR DIARY
or
INTELLIGENCE SUMMARY.

Army Form C. 2118.

Y/29 Trench Mortar Battery.

JANUARY 1919.

Place	Date	Hour	Summary of Events and Information	Remarks and references to Appendices
BERG GLADBACH	1st to 9th		Battery cleaning and painting Guns & wagons. Also Physical training etc.	/c.
	10th to 31st	10.30	N.C.O. R attached for duty to 17th Bde. R.F.A. 1.6.R. N.A.C. & to 29th D.A.H.Q. Remainder of Battery on Physical training to keep Guns & Wagons Newses & Harness in good order.	/ii. /iii.
			Note. From 10th wheel supplies approx. 40% & there have been available for Battery work, Battery worth while for duty	/iv.

G. Priest
Lieut. R.F.A.
O/C Y/29 — T.M.B

Army Form C. 2118.

WAR DIARY
or
INTELLIGENCE SUMMARY
Y/29 Trench Mortar Battery
(Erase heading not required.)

JANUARY 1919.

Place	Date	Hour	Summary of Events and Information	Remarks and references to Appendices
BERG. GLADBACH	1st to 9th		Battery cleaning and painting Guns & wagons &c. Also Physical training etc.	J.S.
	10th to		16.O.R attached for Duty to 17th Bde. R.F.A. 1.O.R attached to 29th D.A.H.Q.	J.S.
	31st		Remainder of Battery on Physical training & keeping Guns & Wagons cleaned & in good order	J.S.
			Note. From 10th inst. crew was approx'ly only 14 men have been available for duty with the battery	J.S.

J.S. Dick
Lieut R.F.A
O/c Y/29 T.M.B

www.ingramcontent.com/pod-product-compliance
Lightning Source LLC
Chambersburg PA
CBHW080831010526
44112CB00015B/2488